"Jesus taught His disciples to pray, 'Thy k
as it is in heaven' (Matthew 6:10 NKJV).
more clearly what this prayer looks like in practice, how such intercession can become
incarnation. All the while, Reyes manages to dismantle the unhelpful and unbiblical
dichotomy between spiritual and material concerns. If you are looking and longing for
tangible, palpable manifestations of the kingdom of God in the time between the times
but do not really know what they would look like if you were to see them, this book is
a must-read. Here, the message is as near as your mouth and heart (so Romans 10:8
citing Deuteronomy 30:14)."

—Todd D. Still, PhD, Charles J. and Eleanor McLerran DeLancey Dean
and William M. Hinson Professor of Christian Scriptures,
Baylor University, Truett Seminary

"It is always a gift to watch God move. Even in the difficult times we live in, God is at work
inspiring, enlightening, and reminding us the harvest is plentiful and the kingdom is near.
Dr. Albert Reyes, in the publication of this masterpiece, has demonstrated that when we are
obedient to God's will, lives can be changed and transformed. This book is indeed a tool
that can change the trajectory of our congregations and communities. He uses Scripture
so eloquently to address the importance of hope for believers and that we must focus on
both the theological and the practical application of the Word in our daily existence. Too
many people are hurting, and in his words, 'The gospel is for the whole person.' The
church cannot suffer more division, and this book can serve as a guide to reconcile the
belief that we must have a sole focus on evangelism or only on social justice. The two must
coexist in a spirit of love for the transformation we seek in our world. Dr. Reyes's work as
CEO of Buckner International demonstrates that this is possible. Lives filled with hope are
evident in the clients and families served. Love is modeled and practiced while needs are
met based on a foundation in Christ and a committed faith walk by Dr. Reyes and the team
he leads with great care and support. I look forward to this book being a catalyst in our
conversations, our churches, and in our communities to show the world Christ in each of
us because of our faith, hope, and love toward one another and all of those we encounter."

—Froswa' Booker-Drew, PhD, director of community affairs
and strategic alliances, State Fair of Texas

"With the Bible as his textbook, Albert Reyes shows us practical ways to lead people to
hope. For Rhonda, an impoverished woman in Kenya, her path started with learning to
bake bread. Ashlee's trail to hope started with grief counseling. Serapio's journey toward
hope involved a class to learn business skills enabling him to provide for his family. For
committed Christ followers, every path to hope intersects at the same place—Jesus. When
talking about the Word becoming flesh, Reyes says, 'It is hard to provide hope from a
distance. Hope is more meaningful when it shows up, when it comes near, in person.' Yes!
Immerse yourself in the stories of lives transformed, and you will be challenged to commit
yourself anew to lead people to Christ who can restore brokenness."

—Sandy Wisdom-Martin, executive director, Woman's Missionary Union

"Three things last forever: faith, hope, and love. Dr. Albert Reyes tackles the importance of hope while explaining the redemptive work required for those working in God's kingdom. This book is not about ministry or religion but about God's kingdom and the hope that provides peace and justice in the world. Albert articulates his journey starting as a pastor doing ministry work to his broken heartedness to serve those who lack hope. Albert's compassion bleeds through the pages of this book as he tells his story that led him to become a leader of hope in this desperate and broken world. Albert's sincerity and passion will stimulate you to follow his example."

—Raymond H. Harris, architect and author of *Business by Design* and *The Heart of Business*

"Albert Reyes's book, *Hope Now: Peace, Healing, and Justice When the Kingdom Comes Near*, guides you through the tensions between an exclusive focus on evangelism over an exclusive focus on social ministry. He aptly wrestles with the differences between physical, emotional, economic, and spiritual needs and how the sum of them represent the *human need*. Then he points to the life of Christ for resolution that brings clarity and the power of hope. Be ready to be challenged about how your life is evidence of the kingdom coming near!"

—Tami Heim, president and CEO, Christian Leadership Alliance

"This is a unique book for several reasons. First, it is based on the real-life experiences Dr. Albert Reyes has had while ministering to people as a pastor, as a university president, and as the CEO of an international benevolence organization. Second, it casts aside the artificial constructs separating evangelism and social ministries and biblically challenges people to follow the example and mandate of the incarnate Jesus Christ himself. Third, its goal is not just to meet the physical needs of the destitute, the orphans, and the marginalized but to transform their lives with the powerful message and compassionate ministry of the gospel of Jesus Christ. The life and ministry of ministers, laypeople, and students will be transformed as they read this challenging and inspiring book."

—Daniel R. Sanchez, distinguished professor of missions, Southwestern Baptist Theological Seminary

"I am very thankful for the blessing of this work authored by Dr. Reyes. Not only is it particularly practical and relevant to this period in church history, it also speaks directly to my ministerial experience over the past three decades. For traditional Baptists like myself, he reminds us of our rich heritage not only of spreading the gospel, planting churches, and establishing conventions but also of meeting the needs of the hurting through medical, orphan, and hundreds of other ministries from the local community to the ends of the earth. This clear call to regain not just the vision of a holistic New Testament commission but to reimplement this vision in light of the example our Savior gave us during His earthly work is a message the church needs to hear."

—Chaplain (CMDR) Bryan Crittendon, United States Navy

HOPE NOW

Peace, Healing, and Justice
When the Kingdom Comes Near

ALBERT L. REYES

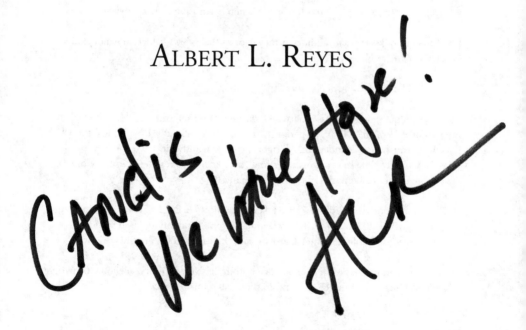

IRON STREAM
BOOKS
An imprint of Iron Stream Media
Birmingham, Alabama

Iron Stream Books
An imprint of Iron Stream Media
100 Missionary Ridge
Birmingham, AL 35242
IronStreamMedia.com

Library of Congress Control Number:2019944365

ISBN-13:978-1-56309-319-7
Ebook ISBN: 978-1-56309-320-3

1 2 3 4 5–23 22 21 20 19

To Dr. Belinda Alvarado Reyes,

My precious wife and partner for the last thirty-seven years. You are a gift to me, my best friend, companion, an amazing mother, research scientist, professor, and my encourager. You have faithfully encouraged me to be the man the Lord intended me to be. Thank you for encouraging me as I wrote this book and for managing without me during extended times of writing and research. Your love for your family is a blessing to us.

> Love is patient, love is kind. It does not envy, it does not boast, it is not proud. It does not dishonor others, it is not self-seeking, it is not easily angered, it keeps no record of wrongs. Love does not delight in evil but rejoices with the truth. It always protects, always trusts, always hopes, always perseveres. Love never fails. . . . And now these three remain: faith, hope and love. But the greatest of these is love.
>
> —1 Corinthians 13:4–8, 13

CONTENTS

GOOD INFORMATION,
GOOD JOURNEYS,
AND GOOD QUESTIONS

After this the Lord appointed seventy-two others and sent them two by two ahead of him to every town and place where he was about to go.

—Luke 10:1

This book flows out of my own journey as a follower of Jesus of Nazareth. I am blessed to have grown up in a family with three generations of faith-filled believers. I understood my need for a Savior and placed my trust and faith in Christ as a nine-year-old boy. Within that year I began talking to my closest friends about matters of faith and led several of them to make the same faith commitment. I cared deeply for them and wanted them to know the good news of forgiveness and salvation found in Jesus Christ. I continued to share this good news with friends and family throughout elementary school, junior high school, high school, and university studies. By the time I arrived at seminary and began theological studies, I was drawn toward courses focused on evangelism, church planting, and missions designed to equip me with skills and tools to do what I had done as a child but in different venues and contexts as an adult.

Most of my pastoral ministry emphasized evangelism, discipleship, church planting, and missions with very little focus on social ministry. I don't recall a time in my pastoral ministry when I was focused on the physical, emotional, or economic well being of people in my circles of influence. My concern focused on their spiritual needs rather than their material needs. While I am deeply indebted and grateful for my experience in seminary, the concept of caring for people in practical ways by looking for solutions to life's most pressing issues like hunger, thirst, injustice, access to resources, access to education, the opportunity to grow up in a family, economic stability, and a long list of items associated with a life of privilege were all foreign concepts to me.

When pastoral ministry needs confronted me with the practical needs of the people I served, I was not equipped to help meet them. My journey to Christ, early experiences in my local church, my experience as a growing disciple of Jesus, my theological training, and my practice as a pastor were missing something, creating a blind spot in my ministry. I was blind to the needs of others and unsure what I could do when faced with the daily struggles of the people I served. Could there be more to faith and practice not only as a pastor but also as a follower of Jesus? What would it mean for the kingdom of God to be real and present in the here and now of my ministry of serving others? What was expected of me as a follower of Jesus and leader in His church? What commands was I to follow serving those in my circle of influence? How would I live out my life as a seeker of God's kingdom?

Across nearly fourteen years of pastoral ministry, seven years in higher education leadership, and more than twelve years of leading Buckner International, I have encountered numerous situations and circumstances to which I was not prepared to respond. In pastoral ministry I regularly encountered transient people, homeless people who sought assistance. I encountered undocumented people, primarily from Mexico and Latin America, who lived in the shadows, separated from their families, struggling to make a living, and sending funds to their struggling families south of the border. I encountered senior adults living in a forgotten, culturally and economically transitional neighborhood. I encountered prostitutes, drug users, gangs, and inner-city violence in the community where I lived and served. I became familiar with the effects of domestic violence and families struggling to survive economically. Confronting the real needs of people in crisis—people desperate for solutions, people lacking basic human needs to survive—became part of my experience as a pastor of a local church in an economically depressed community and in churches that were declining. I met a different kind of reality in those pastoral assignments that was almost entirely new to me, and I felt ill equipped to respond to the needs of those in the church and in the community. I was prepared to respond and provide solutions to spiritual questions and needs on Sunday but was not prepared to respond to needs related to Monday through Saturday. While the churches I served did what they could to respond, such as providing a food bank or a clothes closet, this kind of help only scratched the surface of problems individuals and families struggled with regularly.

In higher education administration, I encountered hundreds of students, many of whom were undocumented, struggling to pay for theological education for a ministry to which they felt called. These students were among the best and brightest for ministry service but had little access to the resources they needed to excel. I felt helpless to respond to their undocumented status while also teaching and training them for a life of ministry. After traveling across Texas, the United States, and other places in the Western Hemisphere like Peru, Guatemala, Honduras, Mexico, the Dominican Republic, and Mexico; in Eastern Europe to places like Moscow and St. Petersburg; to Southeast Asia to places like South Korea, India, and Bangladesh; and to Africa in places like Ethiopia and Kenya, I have seen the deep needs in the lives of people who struggle to live on two dollars a day or less. I have seen poverty and economic instability I never thought were real or possible. I have seen families struggle at deeper levels with basic needs such as food, water, sanitation, and education. I know what it means to offer real-life solutions that make a difference in the here and now while also pointing the way to Jesus and the life He offers now and in the next life. I have witnessed the damage children and families experience when the inability to provide for their families turns fathers and mothers toward drug abuse, alcohol abuse, and physical and sexual abuse, even of their own children. I have witnessed the meltdown of the family unit due to poverty and a lack of access to basic life needs. I am deeply committed through the ministry of Buckner International to build families for children who do not have a family. I am committed to strengthening families with dignity and respect so children can remain in the family in which God placed them for their whole lives. With 150 million orphans in the world, the need seems inexhaustible. I have seen families disintegrate here in the US as well. The need for foster care and adoption has never been greater, and government systems are struggling to respond to the needs of abused, abandoned, and neglected children and their families.

When I looked in my ministry toolbox, I found what I needed to provide good sermons, Bible studies, counseling support, and spiritual development but found very little to address the trauma families were experiencing right in front of me. I knew from a theological perspective the gospel was powerful enough to transform lives and that the Lord Himself as Redeemer could take what was intended for harm and turn it into good. I knew that the Redeemer's kingdom, if it came close enough, would make a difference in the lives of those I was serving, but how did this happen in practical terms?

I don't really know how in traveling through my ministry journey I was so oblivious to the basic needs of the people around me. Perhaps most of the people I grew up with had their basic needs met.

These kinds of needs did not seem to stand out to me as a young man. My theological training did not seem to emphasize human welfare solutions and frameworks to address these issues. Something was missing. The nuts and bolts of practical application of the peace of God and the nearness of the kingdom did not seem to surface in my graduate studies. I accepted my first pastoral assignments with little knowledge and ability to respond to the cries for hope, the desperate needs of hurting people, and the deep wounds of traumatized people.

Am I supposed to help people improve in their living contexts? Is my assignment to share the gospel message and truth about the claims of Christ and the power to transform lives and families? Or am I to do both? And should my focus be limited to individuals and families, or should I be concerned about the whole community and life context? Would the community, the environment, and the city be my focus as well? After all, this is where people live. Is this what pastoral ministry is really about . . . serving people in deep need every day? I observed other pastors who seemed to focus on spiritual issues and delegated meeting physical needs to a staff or church member volunteers. Even the church my wife and I planted in El Paso, Texas, faced some of these same concerns. I could not get away from facing the deep needs people struggle with every day. I felt I was missing something or missed training that would help me see and respond to the genuine needs of people less fortunate than me. I almost felt like this kind of ministry was not my department or responsibility. I later came to realize my view on these issues was limited, uninformed, and inadequate. It did not seem to measure up to the powerful potential of the presence of Jesus, His ability to transform lives, and the impact of the kingdom in the here and now for children, parents, families, and communities where the gospel was preached, taught, heard, and practiced. There seemed to be a gap between the theological and the practical aspects of ministry in my personal experience.

Toward Solutions

My perspective on the spiritual versus the practical began to change when I became president of Hispanic Baptist Theological Seminary (HBTS), now known as Baptist University of the Américas (BUA), in San Antonio, Texas. HBTS was a non-accredited, non-degree granting school, founded in 1947 by San Antonio Baptists for training and equipping Mexican pastors and ministers. I was elected as the sixth president in 1999. About 90 percent of the students were of Hispanic cultural background, many of whom were from Mexico, Central America, and South America. Most of these students had not finished high school, and many were monolingual Spanish-speakers, but all of them sensed a call to vocational ministry. My mission was to lead the school to become an accredited, degree-granting university. By 2003 we were certified by the Texas Higher Education Coordinating Board and accredited by the Association for Biblical Higher Education to grant bachelor of arts degrees and later certified to offer an accredited associate of arts degree for the first time in the school's history. This ministry felt like a cause, a personal mission to provide solutions through higher education that would build bridges for students who were extremely intelligent but lacked the means to obtain a college education for ministry preparation. I was making a tangible difference through meeting the needs of under-resourced, underserved students. I felt I was leading a just cause that was being solved through my efforts and leadership. BUA celebrated its seventieth anniversary in 2017 and continues to graduate bright, bilingual, and bicultural ministry leaders through bachelor and associate degree programs, many of whom have completed graduate studies, obtaining masters and doctoral degrees. These students only needed an opportunity to obtain an education so they could be equipped to lead ministries across the nation as pastors, staff members, and ministry leaders in a wide variety of roles.

My sensitivity toward meeting basic needs of people in ministry leap-frogged when I was called to serve at Buckner International in 2007. In 2010 I was elected the sixth president of this ministry founded in 1879 in Dallas, Texas, to serve vulnerable children, orphans, seniors, and their families. This ministry positioned me right at the feet of vulnerable children who experienced abandonment, abuse, and neglect; with children who became orphans lacking parents and family; and with families who desperately struggled to survive. I felt the Lord called me directly to my blind spots.

It was time for me to stretch even more; to face hard life issues up close and personal; to inspire and lead staff to become the hands and feet of Jesus. This new leadership assignment led me to reexamine the basic teachings of Christ, the difference His incarnational presence made, and the challenge of imitating Him in our daily interactions with people in our community.

I found myself face-to-face with some of the most horrible conditions innocent children could face. I faced situations of neglect, physical, emotional, and sexual abuse, complete abandonment, and a sense of being alone in the world. My heart was broken, but this time I was surrounded by extremely competent and trained social work staff who knew what to do and willingly jumped in to make a difference, to find solutions, and to create healthy family environments where children were loved and could thrive. I wondered if there was a biblical foundation for the kind of ministry I was doing. I wondered what my theological underpinnings would be. I wondered what Jesus had to say about these situations and what He did to transform lives.

What was missing from my theological preparation was a serious and in-depth exposure, review, and study of what the gospel taught about human need; a discovery of the life and work of Jesus with regard to human need; an understanding that the gospel is for the whole of a person and for the communities where they live their everyday life; and a kingdom orientation to the here and now in addition to the yet to be. I was missing the fact that our imitation of Christ in these matters was not to be considered optional. Jesus' commands were not suggestions; rather, Jesus commanded His followers to address human need, to respond to our neighbors with real-life solutions, and to be responsible stewards of our resources and communities. I needed to reset my view of Jesus, reconsider who He was and what He did in order to understand His ministry agenda and what He commands His followers to do and be even today.

The Jesus Agenda

This kind of reflection led me to take a deep theological dive to think about what I was doing in ministry. I began reading about the sermon at the synagogue at Jesus' hometown of Nazareth in the Gospel of Luke and found a powerful and personal mandate He outlined in His first public sermon at the beginning of His thirty-six monthlong ministry. I focused on the redemptive work of Jesus, which was His agenda for His ministry and for human history. I applied those concepts to our work at Buckner International and helped shape our thinking about how and why we do our work. Above all, I concluded we are doing redemptive work. When we meet vulnerable children, orphans, and families in desperate situations, we shine hope into their lives and begin working God's unique plan of redemption for and with them. We become at that point agents of redemption. Clearly Jesus was doing the redemptive work of transforming lives, and we were His agents of redemption.

I wrote a book that spoke that message: *The Jesus Agenda: Becoming an Agent of Redemption.* I began sharing with our staff that when we enter the zone of distress to serve vulnerable children, orphans, and families, we begin to take what was intended for harm and turn it into good as God's redemptive plan for each person we serve. Through this experience and through writing *The Jesus Agenda,* I underwent a sort of ministry-conversion to a new way of thinking about serving others and pursing the kingdom as a priority. I never lost my evangelistic passion and concern for the spiritual needs of people. Rather, I added the other side of the coin of ministry by serving deep needs of desperate people searching for hope. This is the holistic gospel message.

My study led me to conclude every solution set begins with Jesus. It starts with who He was, what He did, how He lived, what He taught, and what He commanded His followers to do. It requires a reexamination of who Jesus is as King; what He brings in His kingdom; what it means to live under the kingship of Christ; what happens when His kingdom comes near; and what it means for us, as followers of Jesus, to follow our King, to live in His kingdom on earth, to be a church that reflects kingdom values, and to be leaders in the kingdom for those we serve. My study in *The Jesus Agenda* led me to understand that Jesus preached, taught, and practiced a holistic style of ministry that addressed not only the spiritual but the physical needs of people. This type of ministry approach was transformational for all those He encountered. This new perspective led me to a more theologically and biblically balanced approach to effective ministry.

False Dichotomy

As I found the other side of the coin of ministry—evangelism on one side and ministering to the needs of people on the other—I became aware of two distinct schools of thought, maybe two distinct philosophies of ministry or two differing theological perspectives. Two camps seem to emerge: those who hyper-focus on evangelism, church planting, and missions through para-church *or* church ministries against those who hyper-focus on meeting personal needs of people in para-church or church ministries almost to the exclusion of a verbal witness. Rarely did I encounter groups that served both ends, both goals, both sides of the coin. I felt like evangelical Christianity fell into two broad categories: evangelistic-oriented groups and social-ministry oriented groups. These two groups usually did not work together and were normally critical of each other. This apparent division may even be more evident in the wider church leading to varying levels of kingdom impact and ineffectiveness. I believe both camps are alive and well today in churches, para-church organizations, and ministries. The problem is they represent a false dichotomy not found in Scripture and not supported in the teachings of Jesus. These two groups operate from only one side of the coin and tend to be oblivious to the notion there is another side. They often do not consider that it is a stewardship to be faithful to or a command of Jesus to be followed.

This journey led me to the Oxford Centre for Mission Studies in Oxford, England, during a sabbatical provided by the board of trustees of Buckner in the summer of 2017 to research and study this very issue. I wanted to learn what Jesus meant when He said "the kingdom has come near," recorded in Luke 10:1–9, and what that might mean for the mission of God through the church, through followers of Jesus, and through you and your family. I wanted to discover what this might mean for the ministry of Buckner International. The gift of a sabbatical from the board of trustees made it possible for me to take a break from the demands of senior executive leadership to think, reflect, and consider the core issues of our ministry related to potential life transformation of those we serve, the incarnational presence of the King and His kingdom in our work, and the reality of the kingdom's nearness as we respond to the most vulnerable, the least of these.

My Question

I wrote this book to rediscover a biblical understanding of Jesus, His life and work, as well as His commands related to a holistic approach to meeting human needs, both spiritual and physical. It is an effort to document the meaning of peace, healing, justice, and the possibility of His kingdom coming near in our lives, in our families, and in our communities. It is my hope that in defining this biblical and Jesus-focused approach to ministry, we might find a sense of unity in evangelical Christianity on these issues. I hope to address clearly the split in our thinking, the false dichotomy, the discontinuity in our theology and practice, and issue a call to unity and to a more biblical, holistic approach to serving others by bringing the kingdom near. This book is an effort to answer key questions that matter today in our hurting world and in our ministry. I admit I am on a journey, an inquiry into the heart of Jesus and His teachings, and I invite you to go with me to explore the meaning of bringing the kingdom near for people around us who need help, hope, and the possibility of a better life, both now and in eternity.

Ultimately, this book seeks to answer this question: Why does evangelical Christianity tend to create a false dichotomy between an exclusive focus on evangelism against an exclusive focus on social ministry? What would an honest reflection of the biblical witness of these two priorities from the life of Jesus tell us? Are these ways of being and doing in conflict or tension with each other? The answer can be found in who Jesus is, what He does, what He brings, and what He demands of His followers as they are sent out into the world. As the concept of the kingdom nearness comes into play, it brings these two polarities in close proximity, expressing two sides of the same coin. Evangelism and social ministry, without the critical component of justice that comes with His kingdom, lead us to fail Christ, His incarnation, His commands, and His kingship.

Truth is found in the commissioning message from our Lord to the seventy-two disciples as found in Luke 10:1–9. The missionary instructions of our Lord point to announcing the kingdom has come near. His instructions serve as a natural expression of the ministry of Jesus, what He embodied through His life and work, what He lived out in practice, and what He now commands those He sent out to do His work.

The missionary instructions given by Jesus bring the whole gospel reality and message. He commands His followers to live out this message as their mission and to announce this kingdom reality. Jesus points their mission toward hope, peace, healing the sick, and inviting justice as His followers enter the harvest of their day. He commands His followers to bring peace, to show that peace through healing, and to bring the kingdom near through these actions.

The evidence of the kingdom coming near in the lives of the seventy-two is clear when they return and give their reports to Jesus. They return with joy, saying even the demons submit to them at the name of Jesus. These followers of Jesus obeyed the commands even among potential threats and dangers as lambs going out among wolves.

As I think about the communities I work with through Buckner International, I agree the harvest is indeed plentiful, but the workers are few. I am intrigued by the presence of Jesus in our work and what His presence might mean for those we serve. I wonder how the peace of Christ might impact vulnerable children, orphans, families, and seniors. I wonder how first-century healing might resonate with vulnerable populations, our families, our churches, and our communities. I wonder what it would mean for the kingdom of Jesus to come near in our work and in our lives as we serve others.

Why This Book Matters

This book is a plea to the next generation of Jesus followers who are already taking on the challenges of our planet by focusing on issues of justice, economic disparity, and opportunity for underserved children, families, and communities not far from where they live and in some cases across the seas. I am writing to young professional men and women who have a passion to make a difference in their generation and who believe they can change the world by doing something. I am writing to the person who wonders how his or her talents, abilities, skills, education, and resources can be used to make a kingdom difference. I am writing to men and women in their twenties, thirties, and forties who desire to seek justice, love mercy, and walk humbly before their God (Micah 6:8).

My hope is that the next generation will capture a vision for ministry and mission as two sides of the same coin, who will discover the Jesus way of holistic ministry and do it. I am writing to those who want to right the things that are wrong in the world like poverty, human trafficking, children living without a family, and families struggling to survive while also telling about the good news of the gospel. I am writing to young professionals who want to change the world in their lifetime and who want to bring the kingdom very near to those who need hope.

During part of this writing I was in Breckenridge, Colorado, on a family vacation. It was the end of May, almost into summer, but two feet of snow fell the day before our arrival, and it snowed two of the three days we were there. Snowing at the end of May in Colorado seemed strange to a family from Texas. It was a surprise to us. Whatever we think should be happening in human history, in redemptive history, it is snowing now. It reminds me that God is in control over everything: the weather, the seasons, human history, even time. We are experiencing a new season of Jesus followers impacting the world around them in intimate ways. We are entering a new season of service, a new season of impact, a new season of blessing, for vulnerable children, struggling families, and seniors. It is a new season of the kingdom coming near and a new season of shining hope. This new season matters because of its intuitional and inspirational potential.

This new season is intuitional because we are leading more with our hearts than heads. Our hearts tell us we need to bring forth real-life solutions for the orphan, the widow, and the alien. We feel the pain of a child extracted from family due to no fault of their own. We feel the pain of children being in "the system" with no family to call their own. We sense the pain of an abused mother who has little hope for the future. We feel the pain of a father who cannot provide for his family. We identify with the pain of the mother who was sexually abused and holds her head down in shame. We can touch the pain of the child who cannot attend school because they do not have a pair of shoes. We know we fall short if we only announce the good news of the gospel. We fail if we only tell about Jesus but don't show the difference He can make. We know things are wrong and need to be made right, right now, in the here and now. We have ample opportunity to share a verbal witness of the hope that is within us when we bring hope to difficult circumstances.

This new season is inspirational because it takes the best of our faith heritage with successes of the past to apply the hope we have in a new way with a new generation of Jesus followers. I am inspired by the potential, the strength, and the power in the hands of the next generation. My hope is they will change the world in ways my generation only dreamed of.

In chapter one I will address my view of our world today and present what the world needs now. In chapter two I lay the foundation for hope found in the person, work, and presence of Jesus, and I will explore how we can engage children, families, and communities in an incarnational way. Chapter three explores how an incarnational approach to hope is most effective when accomplished in community with other followers of Jesus. In chapter four I address what it means to offer hope through peace to children, families, and communities. Chapter five explores how the message of hope and peace becomes a reality in healing relationships, families, and communities. Chapter six examines the notion of hope and justice for vulnerable children, orphans, and their families as a function of the kingdom of Jesus. Chapter seven explains what the kingdom is like, what Jesus taught and practiced about the kingdom, what the early church believed about the kingdom, and how the gospel relates to it. It also explains how lives are transformed and what it means to realize kingdom nearness today as well as in the future. Chapter eight focuses on how the kingdom comes near to me and you.

In the final chapters I intentionally shifted the focus and tone of this book toward a practical application of the first eight chapters to provide a living example of all I have said previously. The last few chapters apply the message of this book in the context of Buckner ministry. Chapter nine imagines what happens when hope shines on vulnerable children, orphans, and families. Chapter ten considers how hope, peace, healing, and justice blend with your kingdom assignment. The conclusion is a glance back to the life of a true kingdom servant: Dr. Robert Cooke Buckner, the visionary founder of the Buckner ministry I currently lead. He was a servant who brought the kingdom near in his time.

Chapter 1

WHAT THE WORLD NEEDS NOW

Now faith is confidence in what we hope for and assurance about what we do not see.

—Hebrews 11:1

When I look back over the first two decades of the twenty-first century, I wonder where our world is going and what we are becoming, and I marvel at how our world is changing over the course of my lifetime. I was born in 1958 and was a child in the 1960s when President John F. Kennedy and Dr. Martin Luther King Jr. were assassinated, the civil rights movement was underway, the sexual revolution redefined so many aspects of culture, and the Vietnam War reshaped our geopolitical landscape. I was a teen in the 1970s when rock and roll and drug use dominated our social fabric, and in the 1980s I went to college, was married, and began my vocation. I watched my world change across the span of my lifetime, but the changes in the first two decades of the twenty-first century feel like our world is rapidly becoming more dangerous, intolerant, and violent.

In the first two decades of the twenty first century . . .

1. Terrorists attacked the World Trade Center and the Pentagon and attempted to attack either the US Capitol or the White House on September 11, 2001.

2. The US invaded Iraq.

3. A tsunami hit Southeast Asia, killing more than 200,000 people in fourteen countries.

4. Hurricane Katrina killed nearly 2,000 people in seven states.

5. North Korea launched its first nuclear test, and Saddam Hussein was executed.

6. Osama bin Laden was hunted down and killed.

7. Terrorist attacks in France, Turkey, California, Belgium, Germany, and London escalated.

8. Tensions between the US and North Korea escalated.

9. Racial tensions, white supremacy, and violence escalated with demonstrations and attacks in Charlottesville, Virginia, and Charleston, South Carolina.

10. In 2017 Hurricanes Harvey, Irma, Lee, and Jose hit coasts throughout the world, devastated communities, and took many lives.

Mass shootings, defined as four or more persons shot and killed by one person in the same general time and place, have become commonplace on the US cultural landscape. Shootings routinely occur in schools, churches, shopping malls, and other public places. In 2017 there were 346 mass shootings in the US, and 340 took place in 2018.[1] The debate and politics of gun regulation have polarized our society while gun violence continues to happen almost weekly.

All this makes the question, and our answer, more urgent: What does our world need now?

What the World Needs Now Is Love, Sweet Love

In 1965 Jackie DeShannon, who grew up in Kentucky, released a song written by Hal David and Burt Bacharach called "What the

---

[1] "Gun Violence Archive 2019," Gun Violence Archive, accessed June 25, 2019, https://www.gunviolencearchive.org/.

World Needs Now Is Love." In 1966 Dionne Warwick picked up the song and recorded it as well. The song calls plaintively for people to love more and hate less. The memorable and engaging melody put a message of compassion in front of the world.

I was intrigued by this song and found that Hal David wrote the lyrics as a prayer to God. It was his attempt to speak for his generation as a cry, a plea to God for more love, not hate.[2] I remember that song. I remember that time.

Yet today, I would not write the same words if I were writing this song. I think I would adapt the words to say that what the world needs now is hope.

Hope in the Storm

A few days after Hurricane Harvey hit the Texas and Louisiana coast in 2017, I traveled with a team of Buckner International leaders to visit children impacted by the storm. These children were evacuated from the Buckner Children's Village in Beaumont, Texas, to Camp Buckner in the Texas Hill Country. As we arrived at the camp, we saw children and families enjoying the experience of camp with games, meals, and fun activities. The scene we encountered was radically different from the experience they left on the Texas coast. On top of abandonment, neglect, and abuse, these children were struggling with major loss. Our team faced the challenge of providing care for trauma-impacted children, which their foster families routinely face. They were also dealing with the visitation of Hurricane Harvey and the destruction and flooding that followed.

I met Janie and her brother at Camp Buckner. Janie was about ten years old. She was removed from her home because her mother

---

[2] Jack Canfield, Mark Victor Hansen, and Jo-Ann Geffen, eds., *The Story behind the Song: The Exclusive Personal Stories behind 101 of Your Favorite Songs.* Chicken Soup for the Soul. (Cos Cob, CT: Chicken Soup for the Soul Publishing), 76–78.

allowed Janie's uncle to come into the home and rape Janie. Her brother, though mentally challenged, knew something was wrong when the he could hear his sister's screams behind a locked door. Janie was among the group of children in foster care evacuated from Beaumont to Camp Buckner. She obviously needed the kind of love that heals her soul, but even before love, she needed hope. She needed hope she would be safe, hope she would not be horrendously violated by her uncle again, hope there would be a better day, a better life.

Hope in the Fire

On a recent trip to Kenya, Africa, I met Janet, a thirty-six-year-old mother of two children, ages four and seven, living in a rented home in Nairobi. When Buckner staff in Kenya first met Janet, she was suffering from a broken heart due to an abusive husband, low self-esteem, poor health, and was literally starving to death with her children. Janet's husband abandoned the family and set her house on fire with Janet and her children in the home, intending to murder them as he left the premises. Janet's neighbors came to her rescue and saved Janet and her children. While Janet survived the fire, she now had to face the challenge of providing for her children as the sole breadwinner for the home. She had no skills, no resources, no financial support, no family, and no plan for providing for her children. She managed to gather a few potatoes and made French fries every evening that she sold in the city, earning less than a dollar a day. This was not enough money to feed her family or pay for her taxi back home to her young children. During those evening efforts to make some money, Janet left her children without a caregiver, hoping a good neighbor would lock them in their home once they fell asleep. This situation further exposed her children to danger. Janet was facing eviction as she was unable to pay her rent.

Janet needed food, financial support, and lots of care. She had no hope that things would improve. She needed a sign of hope. That hope came when a neighbor referred her to Buckner Kenya staff at the Baptist Children's Center (BCC) in Nairobi. Our staff attended to her needs through an assessment, psychological care, health care, and nutrition for her and her children. She began family coaching with Buckner and developed a plan for how to sustain her family. Prior to meeting Buckner staff, Janet was alone and isolated in the community. In addition to her physical, psychological, and economic needs being met, she was introduced to members of the local church who welcomed her into the community of faith.

Today, Janet is the lead member of the worship and praise group in her church and serves as church secretary of the Merciful Gospel Church in Nairobi. Through family coaching at the Buckner Family Hope Center at the BCC, Janet learned new skills and now earns a living through selling cakes and snacks at the local bus station during peak hours. She started a new business with a capital loan of twenty US dollars and a loan from a local banking group. She was able to save enough money to start a poultry business where she raises chickens and sells eggs. These business enterprises enable her to sustain her family and provide for her children's needs. She found hope. She found solutions. She found a family of faith who loved and accepted her. The smile on her face and confidence she carried in her walk came from a deep sense of hope for the future. What Janet needed was hope.

Hope amidst a Total Meltdown

I met Emily, a forty-one-year-old widow, mother of five, and grand-mother of two, at her home in Kitale, Kenya. After visiting the Reynolds Medical Clinic at the Buckner Family Hope Center in Kitale, my team traveled a few miles to Emily's home on her farm.

Emily lives in a one-room, mud-walled, grass-thatched round house on less than an acre of land with her children. She lacked confidence, self-esteem, and the ability to care for herself, her children, and her grandchildren, barely living on a subsistence income. The trauma and vulnerability of Emily's situation wore her down to the point of hopelessness for her future. She suffered mentally and displayed abnormal behavior. At one point she abandoned her home and land. She became physically destructive and was isolated from her community.

Her neighbors contacted the Buckner Family Hope Center in Kitale for assistance. Emily agreed to participate in an assessment of her condition. The assessment demonstrated high risk factors for her and her family. After beginning classes she began to show some improvement but continued to develop abnormal behavior due to her condition. The Buckner team intervened with counseling, medication, and spiritual support through prayers. She was referred to the county psychiatric hospital and after some time began to show improvement. Right before graduation she digressed again and halted her participation in the program. She was readmitted to the Kitale District Hospital psychiatric department and eventually to the Moi Teaching and Referral Hospital in Eldoret. Two months later, after plenty of rest and treatment, Emily was released and returned home.

She reentered the Buckner Family Hope Center program with enthusiasm and a new sense of hope. She identified farming as her greatest interest and began planting and selling seedlings. She was able to save money to develop additional capital and expand her farming operation. She joined a local savings and loan organization to gain access to more capital to expand her business. Emily has been healed on many levels.

After our visit with Emily, I presented a wooden cross to her and asked if I could say a prayer for her and her family. She agreed with a smile on her face. We held hands and formed a circle and thanked God for healing her and restoring her to her home. When I opened my eyes after my prayer I saw Emily had let go of the hand of the person next to her and had raised it to the sky as a symbol of praise to God for all He had done. Emily had experienced a meltdown, and she needed hope. She now attends a local church where she participates in Bible study, prayer, and worship and has access to hope every week.

Hope amidst Chaos and Uncertainty

Amanda is a fourteen-year-old young lady living in Dallas, Texas. She and her family are part of the 82,000 people who live in the three-square-mile area just north of Love Field in Dallas known as the Bachman Lake community. When the air traffic is busiest, planes fly across the area every two minutes, and they're a regular occurrence throughout the day. Bachman Lake is home to more children under the age of five than any other area, and many of them live either in poverty or under the constant threat of economic instability. Fifty-seven percent of residents have less than a high school education, limiting their job opportunities and earning power. The Child Protective Services removal rate in Bachman is twice the Dallas County average.

Amanda knows the threats all too well. She sees them each time she walks out the door of the one-bedroom apartment she shares with her parents and five siblings. Men loiter in the parking lot. Some sell drugs. Others consume alcohol through the day. Gang activity and drug trade is common. In early 2018 five shootings took place, including one that wounded a nine-year-old boy. Young women can be found selling themselves at a nearby gas station. Such activity only increases when the sun goes down.

In this environment, it's easy for families to fail. The stress of poverty weighs heavily on them and affects parents' relationships with each other and with their children. Amanda's family nearly collapsed in 2017. Serapio, Amanda's father and sole financial provider for the family, lost his job, leaving the family in financial chaos, with the prospect of homelessness looming over their heads. The financial stress led to a level of impatience on the part of Amanda's mother, Marta. She began to lose hope for her family.

Amanda's parents started making piñatas and selling them through a broker to get by financially. Her father went to the banks of the Trinity River near downtown Dallas to cut bamboo as raw material for piñatas to build the skeletons and cover them with colored paper. They sold their piñatas for fifteen dollars each to a distributor who would sell them at a higher price. It was better than nothing but not enough to sustain the family. Amanda's family began losing hope they could survive after a job loss and very little income.

Marta and Serapio began taking classes at the Buckner Family Hope Center in the Bachman Lake community. In those classes, they learned how to create a business plan and how to market their piñatas, taking advantage of larger opportunities to sell their products. As a result, the couple started earning more than double what they were earning when selling each piñata. The income helped the family get by until Amanda's father found another job. Now, the piñatas supplement Serapio's paycheck to save for a down payment on a house.

Amanda is an excellent student in a college-preparatory program at Thomas Jefferson High School where she'll earn an associate degree at the same time she receives her high school diploma. Her dream is to become the first college graduate in her family and eventually become an elementary math teacher. She hopes to be an example to her brothers and not give up on life. Amanda and her family needed hope and the possibility things would get better.

Hope in a Life-Threatening Situation

Tilia was fourteen years old when she was diagnosed with polycystic kidney disease, the same disease that took her mother and grandmother. In 2017 Tilia, a wife and mother of three beautiful girls in the Bachman Lake community, was diagnosed with stage 5—end-stage renal disease. This news was shocking and unexpected to Tilia, causing her to hide from the rest of the world. Often sitting in the dark, she avoided her friends and found herself spiraling into despair with no hope for a future. All she could do was cry and ask herself, "Why?" She recalls thinking about the memories of her mom going through the disease. And it made her not want to do anything with the outside world. She lost all hope and did not know what to do other than to pray and ask God for help.

She had no hope until she met Ricardo Brambila, the director of the Buckner Family Hope Center at Bachman Lake. Her friends began to lift her up and practically dragged her to the first class. Tilia recalls the class being full of energy and encouragement. She enjoyed it, and she wanted more. Eventually, Tilia began taking three different classes at the Family Hope Center. Buckner staff invested in her, helping her look at the positive aspects of her life.

Through spiritual development activities, Buckner staff offered her a Bible and prayer. I led a team of staff, including Sabrina Sariles and Juan Valdez, on the first visit to her home. We knocked on the door to her apartment, and she answered.

"Hi, my name is Albert Reyes. This is Sabrina and Juan. We have come to deliver the Bible you requested," I said.

I expected to remain outside her apartment, but she welcomed us in. Her three daughters were working on homework assignments, and her husband was at work. We stood in the entryway of her apartment and began our conversation.

"What would you like for us to pray about?" I asked.

She took a deep breath, her eyes began to water, and she began to wring her hands.

"I have a life-threatening medical condition with my kidneys," she said.

She described her illness while also wiping away big tears welling up in her eyes. I felt helpless, and all I could do was offer to pray for healing.

"We believe God can heal you through lots of different ways, so would you like to ask Him now about your condition?" I asked.

She immediately agreed and interrupted her girls from their homework and ushered them close to pray with us. The girls quickly joined us in a circle to pray for Tilia. We held hands while I explained we were going to talk directly to God about their mom and ask Him to heal her body and give her a long life. I offered the best prayer I could with deep and sincere words to Jehovah Rapha, the God who heals, on Tilia's behalf. After the prayer, I could see a sense of relief in Tilia's eyes. That prayer was the beginning of a new sense of hope.

Despite her medical situation, Tilia began striving for herself and her family. When she began taking a class about how to start a business, she knew she found what she and her husband Ricardo were missing. The couple previously talked about starting a company for years. Ricardo was part of home construction teams and an expert in the field but wanted to start his own business with his wife. All they needed was training on how to start. Tilia sensed the timing was right for her family to start a business.

For weeks they cut every expense they could, even going to a church food pantry for food, so they could save enough money to purchase the tools Ricardo needed for a construction business. The family was encouraged in their effort to start a business, knowing Buckner staff believed in them. With the help of Buckner, the family knew they would succeed. In three weeks they started their own business. The business is growing each day as Ricardo has found work in the far northern suburbs of Dallas. He and his staff work from sunrise to sunset each day constructing homes. The business's success has alleviated the financial stress upon the family.

Tilia still struggles with her illness, and we continue to pray for healing. She's waiting on a kidney transplant and takes twenty pills a day. But she looks forward to each new day with a new belief in herself.

"I can now set goals for myself that I know I can accomplish because I have great people who help me with them," she said.

Tilia's medical condition has not been resolved, but her perspective has changed. Her faith in Christ has provided a firm foundation for the future. She found hope. She can dream again.

Hope is what is on the minds and hearts of people we serve through the ministries of Buckner. What people want when they face impossible circumstances and the pain of loss, betrayal, violence, abuse, neglect, and abandonment is hope. They long for a better life, and they hope things might get better. In Paul's letter to the Corinthians, he writes, "Three things will last forever—faith, hope, and love" (1 Corinthians 13:13 NLT).

John Eldredge, an author, counselor, and teacher, says in his book *All Things New*, "Hope is the wind in your sails, the spring in your step. Hope is so essential to your being that Scripture calls it 'an anchor for the soul' (Hebrews 6:19)."[3] Eldredge goes on to illustrate how people who battle cancer or other diseases realize hope is essential for survival. People who go through a painful divorce know how hope is the lifeline for a meaningful future. And people who suffer in poverty know how critical hope is in overcoming tough

[3] John Eldredge, *All Things New: Heaven, Earth, and the Restoration of Everything You Love* (Nashville: Nelson Books), 8.

circumstances. He says that once you abandon hope, your body gives up the fight: "Faith is something that looks backward . . . Love is exercised in the present moment . . . Hope looks forward, anticipating the good that is coming. Hope reaches into the future to take hold of something we do not yet have, may not even see."[4]

What is on your heart today as you read these words and consider the condition of your family, neighbors, coworkers, and friends and as you consider the condition of our cities, counties, country, and world? Is faith, hope, or love the priority of your heart today? I can tell you firsthand that people who are hurting need hope the most. What the world needs now is hope, sweet hope.

Questions to Consider

Is there a situation in your life that moves you to the point of needing hope for the future, for a better future?

What do you need hope for that you cannot see today or in the foreseeable future?

---

[4] Ibid, 9.

Who in your circle of influence needs hope that things will get better for themselves and their family?

Is there a promise you can find in the Bible that speaks to a situation that requires hope?

What can you point to in the Christian faith that promises the potential of hope for you, your family, or those in your circle of influence?

Chapter 2

HOPE IS INCARNATIONAL

The Word became flesh and made his dwelling among us.

—John 1:14

Hope starts with Jesus of Nazareth.

The first and most powerful thing Jesus ever did was invade our space, to break into human history. He came to earth as a baby born in a manger in the first century. Before the first Christmas, before his presentation at the Temple, a Temple disappearance, his baptism, ministry, miracles, trial, Crucifixion, Resurrection, and ascension, God *decided* to come very near through Jesus. He thought about us. He knew we needed hope. Then he came to us. It is hard to provide hope from a distance. Hope is more meaningful when it shows up, when it comes near, in person. John, the Gospel writer, says that before time existed, in the beginning was the Word, Jesus. Jesus, the Word, was with God. He also said Jesus was God (John 1:1). In the very beginning, before human history, Jesus existed. He was with God. He was God. The rest of this book could be spent exploring that one truth. If you miss this one fact, you may not understand anything else I am writing about.

The part of John's account that is critical to grasp is that hope, in the form of a person, came near. John wrote, "The Word became flesh." He became flesh and blood. He became human. He was God in human form. He pitched His tent, so to speak, among us. John said, "We have seen his glory, the glory of the one and only Son, who came from the Father, full of grace and truth" (v. 14). John was not describing a dream, a vision, or his imagination. What he was saying was he saw Jesus, up close and in person. Jesus was incarnate. He was present and near. He brought hope. He showed up in person. Jesus is not an idea of philosophy. Rather, He is God's visual aid because He is God Himself. When Jesus shows up, He brings hope.

To unwrap this powerful truth, one must explore who Jesus was and is. We must also explore what Jesus did. As you know, actions speak louder than words. We must also explore what Jesus commanded and consider what it means to imitate Him, to live out life in the kingdom.

Who Jesus Is

Who is Jesus? It feels impossible to answer. Yet to understand hope as incarnational, this question must be fleshed out. Scripture is probably the best place to start.

At an Easter celebration in April 2015, Matt Fry, founding pastor of C3 Church in Clayton, North Carolina, preached "Hope's Name Is Jesus," a message listing Jesus in all the books of the Bible. He mentioned the name of Jesus from all sixty-six books of the Bible. Some of the more likely examples included Jesus as Creator in Genesis, Jesus as the Passover Lamb in Exodus, and Jesus as Redeemer in the Book of Ruth. You may not think of Jesus as the Mediator between God and man in Job or the Author of love in Song of Solomon. Fry closed his sermon with the idea that hope's name is Jesus![5] The name of Jesus is found throughout the witness of Scripture, which is full of specific details of His background.

The Gospel of Luke records Jesus was born of Jewish parents, Joseph and Mary, who traveled from their hometown of Nazareth, a town in Galilee, to Bethlehem, the city of King David, to give

---

[5] Matt Fry, "Hope's Name Is Jesus," C3 Church, accessed February 7, 2019, https://c3church.com/messages/hopes-name-is-jesus/.

birth to their firstborn son, Jesus. Luke notes Jesus was born in a manger with shepherds attending His birth (Luke 2:1–20). Jesus grew up in Nazareth and launched His ministry there with His first public sermon at the synagogue He attended as a child and young man (Luke 4:14–30). Jesus of Nazareth lived, served, died, and was Resurrected from the dead. He appeared to many of His disciples after His death.[6] Jesus has been portrayed in movies with a British accent or by an actor having European descent. The reality was that Jesus was of Middle-Eastern descent, a Jew. As the Resurrected Son of God, He is Creator, Lord, Redeemer, Savior, who lives and reigns and will return at some point in the future of human history. Jesus is God, and God is passionately interested in a personal relationship with you. He wants you to know Him, and He wants you to learn and do His purpose for your life. Any effort to know who Jesus is would include an understanding of what He did while on earth.

What Jesus Did

In October 2000 Damien Cave, a writer for *Salon,* addressed a question that has become a staple in Christian culture: What would Jesus do? "Long before the words 'What would Jesus do?' became a bumper-sticker staple, thirty-five teenagers in a religious youth group in Holland, Michigan, proposed to make the question a central part of their lives. They promised their youth group leader, Janie Tinklenberg, they would ask it before every decision, following the example of the characters in *In His Steps,* a century-old collection of sermons that Tinklenberg was fond of citing."[7]

---

[6] See these instances of Jesus appearing to His disciples: Matthew 28:5–7, 11–15, 16–17; Mark 16:5–7; Luke 24:4–8, 33–37; John 20:1–2, 19–20; John 21:14; Acts 1:9–12; and 1 Corinthians 15:3–7.

[7] Damien Cave, "What Would Jesus Do—About Copyright?" *Salon,* October 25, 2000, https://www.salon.com/2000/10/25/wwjd/.

The year was 1989. Tinklenberg was searching for a way to keep the initials WWJD in front of her youth group. She thought T-shirts would not do because they could be discarded. She thought of WWJD bracelets, and the rest is history. But even before Tinklenberg came up with the idea, a Congregationalist minister named Charles Sheldon, born in Topeka, Kansas, came up with a sermon series in the 1890s intended to entice his members to come to church on Sunday nights. He published his sermons in a Congregationalist magazine in 1896, and they were then compiled and published as a book, *In His Steps*.

Cave—and Tinklenberg—pointed out that the issue of WWJD is not the question itself but the answers that are given and how grappling with faith leads to them.[8] If our answers are left up to us and our imagination, we can stray away from who Jesus was and what He did.

Can we really know what Jesus would do? We can only know what He did. If WWJD is intended to be a prompt or a reminder, it may be a good slogan. But I don't think WWJD is the best question. We know what Jesus did by our examination of Scripture. Once we know what He did, we can apply principles that help us know what we should do.

My purpose here is not to write everything Jesus did. Even John, the Gospel writer, admitted he was not able to record all Jesus did during His earthly ministry. The last verse in the Gospel according to John says, "Jesus did many other things as well. If every one of them were written down, I suppose that even the whole world would not have room for the books that would be written" (John 21:25).

What was Jesus all about? N. T. Wright suggests the first century movement called Christianity believed Jesus to be the Davidic

---

[8] Ibid.

King promised long ago. In other words, God was now in charge through Jesus. God's kingdom, through Jesus, was launched in the first century.[9] Wright says, "From the moment Jesus launched His public career, He seems to have been determined to speak about God Himself becoming king. He announced that God's kingdom was now at hand. He commands His hearers to give up their dreams and to trust His instead. This, at its simplest, is what Jesus was all about."[10] What Jesus was all about framed what He did.

Jesus was all about establishing God's rule on earth. But the way He went about bringing this truth to life was unique. Jesus set up His earthly kingdom as a servant.[11] He said of Himself, "For even the Son of Man did not come to be served, but to serve, and to give his life as a ransom for many" (Mark 10:45). The miracles of Jesus are like a headline that shows God is at work. He worked miracles not to show His authority but to point to the reality of the kingdom already amid Israel.[12] He taught the good news of the kingdom through parables. He taught and preached about the kingdom as a summons to those who heard Him. He was calling people to Himself and to His kingdom.[13] He taught in order to reveal what God's kingdom meant and to say it was present and ongoing.

The reality of the kingdom in Jesus' preaching was first announced in His hometown of Nazareth in the synagogue. Reading from the prophet Isaiah, Jesus outlined His agenda for His ministry: to bring

---

[9] N. T. Wright, *Simply Jesus: A New Vision of Who He Was, What He Did, and Why He Matters* (New York: Harper Collins Publishers, 2011), 54–55.

[10] Ibid., 56.

[11] Arthur Glasser, Charles Edward van Engen, Dean Gilliland, and Shawn B. Redford, *Announcing the Kingdom: The Story of God's Mission in the Bible* (Grand Rapids: Baker Publishing Group, 2003), 187.

[12] Ibid., 188.

[13] Ibid., 186.

the rule of His kingdom near for the poor, the blind, the oppressed, and the imprisoned and to announce the year of the Lord's favor.[14] Wright says the "year of our Lord's favor" was a reference to the year of Jubilee when all debts were eliminated and ownership was transferred to the original owner. The coming of the kingdom announced by Jesus provided a tangible example of God's attitude toward poverty and injustice. Wright calls the sermon Jesus preached in the synagogue Jesus's "Nazareth Manifesto." He refers to the year of Jubilee as the Sabbath of all Sabbaths, "a rescue from all that has crippled human life."[15] Jesus taught about serving the poor, providing healing and relief. Beyond teaching, He practiced what He preached and taught.

Jesus demonstrated the reality of God's reign, the kingdom, through His life and brief ministry. He did so much in His life but even more through His death. His death on a Friday afternoon on a Roman cross is the crucial and central point in human history. Yet human history is not large enough to frame what Jesus did. N. T. Wright makes a case for Jesus' death to be placed in a broader context, redemptive history, God's redemptive work in the world. Wright argues that "according to the book of Revelation, Jesus died in order to make us not rescued nonentities, but restored human beings with a vocation to play a vital part in God's purposes for the world."[16] Wright says our view of Jesus's death on the Cross as focused solely on the goal of securing our salvation and forgiveness of our sins falls short of what first-century followers of Jesus believed and understood. The death of Jesus on a Cross started a "revolution"

---

[14] See Luke 4:14–30, and for a broader explanation, see my book *The Jesus Agenda: Becoming an Agent of Redemption*. (Colorado Springs: Believers Press, 2015).

[15] Wright, *Simply Jesus*, 74.

[16] N. T. Wright, *The Day the Revolution Began: Reconsidering the Meaning of Jesus's Crucifixion* (New York: Harper Collins, 2016), 5.

according to Wright. Jesus lived a revolutionary life, presented revolutionary teachings, and died a revolutionary death. Would it not make sense that what He commanded His followers to do was also revolutionary, even countercultural?

What Jesus Commanded

The commands of Jesus, as I have heard them preached and taught throughout my life, are often focused on two key passages in Scripture: the Great Commission found in the Gospel of Matthew 28:19–20 and the Great Commandment in Matthew 22:37–40. I am focusing on the Great Commission first since it has historically been given prominence in my spiritual development and training, even though it is found in the last chapter of Matthew's Gospel. The Great Commission is often quoted as the primary focus of all Jesus commanded. The command is given following the Resurrection of Jesus from the dead. He gathered His eleven disciples in Galilee on a mountain where Jesus instructed them to meet Him. When they saw their risen Lord, they worshipped Him, but there were a few who doubted. Jesus approached them and declared He had all authority on earth and in heaven. Given that declaration, Jesus said: "Therefore go and make disciples of all nations, baptizing them in the name of the Father and the Son and the Holy Spirit, and teaching them to obey everything I have commanded you."

Priority is often placed on these actions: making disciples and baptizing, often thought of as evangelism and discipleship. The third action is not always emphasized: "Teaching them to obey everything I have commanded you." The action of "teaching them to obey" is a longer and more challenging process of teaching, training, imitating, mentoring, and coaching, all folded into the process of discipleship and spiritual maturity. The best context for this is an interpersonal relationship between a mature follower of Jesus and a newcomer to the faith. While there are many models and tools for life-on-life discipleship, the best material I have used in pastoral ministry was developed by Thom Wolf called The Pattern.[17] I used this pattern as a pastor leading new followers of Jesus to learn how to live like Jesus, and I incorporated The Pattern as part of a leadership course at Baptist University of the Américas. Discipleship is the precursor to Christian leadership. How can leaders lead in the kingdom if they have not mastered how to follow Jesus?

The second major command is the Great Commandment found in Matthew 22:37–40. Jesus was tested by the religious establishment, teachers of the Mosaic Law. One of the expert teachers of the Law asked Jesus this question: "Teacher, which is the greatest commandment in the Law?" Jesus replied, "'Love the Lord your God with all heart and with all your soul and with all your mind.' This is the first and greatest commandment. And the second is like it: 'Love your neighbor as yourself.' All the Law and the Prophets hang on these two commandments."

Two major truths jump out. First, I see the simplicity of Jesus' commands: Love the Lord your God and love your neighbor as yourself. You might boil it down even more like this: Love God; love your neighbor. It's that simple. Albert Schweitzer notes the ethic of love for one's neighbor also extends to one's enemy.[18] He cites Matthew 5:43–45 where Jesus teaches, "You have heard that it was said, 'Love your neighbor and hate your enemy.' But I tell you, love your enemies and pray for those who persecute you, that you may be

---

[17] Thom Wolf, "The Pattern: God's DNA for Living," Thom Wolf University Institute Educational Edition, New Delhi, India, 2014. Originally developed by Thom Wolf as "The Universal Discipleship Pattern," The Global Spectrum, New Delhi, India, 1992.

[18] Albert Schweitzer, *The Kingdom of God and Primitive Christianity* (New York: Seabury Press, 1968), 85.

children of your Father in heaven." Schweitzer also points out how the "ethic of love" extends to the love of foreigners, citing Leviticus 19:33 as a means for seeking the kingdom of God on earth.[19] This idea of Jesus seems unfamiliar to those who follow Him while also placing a higher value on nationalism, especially in the United States of America in our current geopolitical climate. Allegiance to the United States of America may possibly compete with allegiance to the kingdom of God regarding issues of immigration and border security. A balance of perspectives on national security and the Jesus ethic of loving the foreigner is a challenging task for those who claim Jesus as King.

The equally astonishing principle Jesus teaches here is that all the teachings of the Mosaic Law and the teachings of the Old Testament prophets depend or hang on these two commandments. Jesus went beyond the frame of the question of the teachers of the Law. He summarized the teaching from the Law of Moses and the teaching of the prophets like Isaiah, Jeremiah, Hosea, Amos, Micah, Habakkuk, and Malachi. The cumulative teaching of *all* the prophets, major and minor prophets, depend on these two commandments: Love God; love your neighbor. The commands are bidirectional. That is, they vertically define a proper relationship with God, and they horizontally define our relationship with other people.

Love God and love your neighbor is the basic teaching. However, a closer exploration of all the commands Jesus gave His followers leads to the deeper riches of wisdom and guidance for living. Start with the commands of Jesus. Examine them. Consider how they would be applied to your life. Find a seasoned follower of Jesus to shape, coach, mentor, and model these commands for you. These teachings echo through twenty-one centuries and form the basis for

---

[19] Ibid., 86.

the best way "to live life on the planet."[20] When you engage the teachings of Jesus and begin to apply them to your life, you will join the global conversation[21] that poses this question: What is the best way to live life on the planet?

The Fifty Commands of Jesus

I came across a list of fifty commands of Jesus. The compiler split the list of commands in two. Half of the commands are teachings applicable for "all peoples and times" in the universal sense of the word.[22] David Cook says the ethics of Jesus has universal appeal among peoples of all faiths.[23] The other half, while somewhat applicable universally, are uniquely applicable to devoted followers of Jesus.

Jesus masterfully tied the ethical teachings of the Old Testament with what He taught as recorded in the New Testament. However, to say Jesus came to teach a "new ethic," a new way of living, is to misunderstand Him and His mission. The ethics of Jesus are rooted in the ethical teaching of Judaism, in the Law and Prophets as John Bright points out when he says what set Jesus apart from the ethical teachings of Judaism was His "summons to radical obedience which we seldom or never find among Jewish teachers."[24] Bright argues for a seamless fabric between the Old and New Testaments while also contending for a "new thing" in the teachings of Jesus bound

---

[20] Ibid.

[21] See Thom Wolf, "The Global Conversation," at www.universityinstitute.in.

[22] Lance Wallnau, "50 Commands of Christ," accessed February 7, 2019, http://www.servingourneighbors.org/uploads/1/8/3/2/18326231/50_commands_of_christ-revised.pdf.

[23] David Cook, *Living in the Kingdom: The Ethics of Jesus*. (London: Hodder & Stoughton, 1992), 3–4.

[24] John Bright, *The Kingdom of God: The Biblical Concept and Its Meaning for the Church* (Nashville: Abingdon Press, 1953), 194.

together by the "dynamic concept of the rule of God . . . the kingdom of God."[25] But what does this mean for us today? How do our lives connect with Jesus and His kingdom now? How do we imitate Jesus in the twenty-first century in a globally connected world that needs hope? How does the teaching of Jesus to "love God and love our neighbor" intersect with our lives, our families, our faith community, our local church, or Christian ministry? How might we live out the kingdom life today?

Imitating Jesus: Living out the Kingdom Life

Throughout my life I learned about Jesus. As a child I learned "Jesus loves me, this I know. For the Bible tells me so. Little ones to Him belong. They are weak, but He is strong. Yes! Jesus loves me. Yes, Jesus loves me. Yes! Jesus loves me. The Bible tells me so." I learned who He is, what He did, and what He commanded. I knew His teachings applied to me, personally. I knew I was expected to live up to His standards of right living. I learned the ethics of Jesus in my home when I was younger from my parents who taught me the Bible, took me to church and Bible study, and nurtured me spiritually. I took a course in seminary on Christian ethics. I learned about the kingdom of God too, but not as deeply as I now understand it. But something happened to me in the last few years. The teachings of Jesus, the ethics of Jesus, and the understanding of the kingdom met in one place in my heart, soul, and mind. Honestly, I must confess I never thought of these topics together. I had not considered them in an interdependent way.

Now, I can't see them without seeing them together in relationship. I see them at intersections of life and faith; life and work; and life and family. My experiences were leading me this way. I was beginning to

---

[25] Ibid., 197.

connect theological and biblical synapses in my brain. I was moved in my heart. In the few weeks at the Oxford Centre for Mission Studies in Oxford, England, in the summer of 2017, I read Dr. David Cook's book *Living in the Kingdom*. I found I could not put it down. Cook succinctly made the case for living in the kingdom. This was a watershed moment for me. What I had experienced came together in this one volume.

Cook contends that all ethical living is connected to being loved by God. There is no separation between religion and ethics in Christianity. He maintains that good theology leads to good living. If not, there is something wrong with your theology. He calls this kingdom living.[26] To live in the kingdom is to obey Jesus the King.

Bright argues that to be a member of Christ's kingdom, one must obey his teachings. This means feeding the hungry, clothing the naked, showing mercy to the prisoner and outcast. These actions in response to the summons of the kingdom of God are the way we show we understand the ethics of Jesus found in the New Testament.[27]

It is tempting to project the ethical teachings of Jesus as a way of life for the general population or society or as a program to reform society. Jesus did not bring a new way of living, though, to reform society. He brought a new ethic to "summon men (and women) to the kingdom of God and its righteousness."[28] Jesus intended for His teachings and commands to be taken seriously by His followers. The ethics of Jesus are the ethics of the kingdom of God[29] and set the community of the King apart from the general population. The teachings of Jesus and the kingdom way of life are the responsibility

---

[26] Cook, *Living in the Kingdom*, 12.

[27] Bright, *The Kingdom of God*, 221.

[28] Ibid., 222.

[29] Ibid.

of every Christian. That is, to do the will of God. Doing the will of God brings the kingdom near.[30] As obedience to the will of God and the teachings of Jesus begins to happen in the life of a follower of Jesus, the kingdom is evident. Things begin to change. Relationships change. Families are impacted. Communities begin to transform. The culture begins to shift. Followers of Jesus in the community imitate Jesus and the kingdom way. The community begins to be a place where the kingdom resides. The King and His kingdom come near.

One example is the abolition of slavery in the early 1800s in England. William Wilberforce and Antony Ashley Cooper, later Lord Shaftesbury, worked together to change the British industrial enterprise and its conditions. They eventually led the movement to abolish slavery in England. They were evangelical Christians working together to bring the kingdom near.[31] Followers of Jesus in the first century were known for living out the teachings of Jesus. Rodney Stark reconstructed a sociological perspective of the growth of early Christianity and shows how a tiny, obscure messianic movement grew from about one thousand followers to over thirty-three million adherents over a period of three hundred years. He asks why and how this movement called Christianity grew so astronomically.[32] Among the reasons Stark shows how maintaining open social networks and structures for direct and intimate interpersonal relationships made the spread of the good news and life transformation possible.[33] Another example

---

[30] Cook, *Living in the Kingdom*, 13.

[31] Ibid., 26.

[32] Rodney Stark, *The Rise of Christianity: How the Obscure, Marginal Jesus Movement Became the Dominant Religious Force in the Western World in a Few Centuries* (Princeton: Princeton University Press, 1996), 3–7.

[33] Ibid., 20.

of Christians living out kingdom ethics was recorded during the second great epidemic in Rome in the year 260. Dionysius, Bishop of Alexandria, wrote an Easter letter. His letter documented the heroic nursing efforts of Christians, many of whom lost their lives while caring for others.[34]

In the Graeco-Roman world, the female mortality rate was very high due to the high rate of infanticide and abortion, a practice discouraged by the subculture of Christianity. Stark demonstrates how the earliest Christians in the first few centuries of the Graeco-Roman world revitalized their cities and provided sustainable solutions. To homeless and impoverished people, Christianity offered charity and hope. To cities filled with newcomers and strangers, Christianity offered circles of relationships and community. To cities filled with orphans and widows, Christianity provided a new meaning of extended family. To cities torn by violent ethnic strife, Christianity offered a new basis for social solidarity. To cities impacted by epidemics, fires, and earthquakes, Christianity offered effective nursing services.[35] It is clear the earliest followers of Jesus in the first few centuries of Christianity took their faith seriously and imitated the ways of Jesus. They were countercultural, adding value to their communities and society. The monastic movement with its focus on good works, spiritual life, and meeting human needs is another example of life in Christ that was countercultural. But what about us today? How are we to live in the twenty-first century given all the social upheaval and deterioration of social structures and biblical norms?

Paul the apostle encouraged followers of Jesus to imitate him: "Therefore I urge you to imitate me. For this reason I have sent to

[34] Ibid., 82.
[35] Ibid., 161.

you Timothy, my son whom I love, who is faithful in the Lord. He will remind you of my way of life in Christ Jesus, which agrees with what I teach everywhere in every church" (1 Corinthians 4:16–17) What is fascinating to me is that Paul, an apostle of Jesus, writing to the Christians in Corinth, sends Timothy like a word-picture for them to imitate. Timothy is yet another visual aid for the way of life in Christ. What qualifies Timothy is that he is faithful. He is qualified to show the Corinthian Christians the way of life in Christ Jesus. There was a teaching or a pattern of teaching for how to imitate Jesus that Paul taught. Note that he taught this pattern everywhere and in every church.[36] The pattern of living in the kingdom, the Jesus way, can be discovered. The pattern of living according to the ethics of Jesus can be imitated. It is possible for you and me. It is within our reach. We can continue throughout this century to demonstrate what it means to live by the commands of Jesus. We can live by the ethic of love. We can live in the kingdom now.

My goal in this chapter was to show how the hope the world needs now starts with Jesus. To understand that hope we must first understand who Jesus is. We must explore what He did. We must know what He commanded His followers. We must consider what it means to imitate Jesus today. We must imitate the first Christians as they imitated Jesus. This is what it means to do kingdom living. What does that really look like today? The next chapter will explore this idea more fully. We will consider what hope looks like in the community of faith, in the community of Jesus, in the community of the kingdom.

---

[36] See Thom Wolf, The Global Conversation, at www.universityinstitute.in.

Questions to Consider

In your own words, who is Jesus?

What did He do?

What did He command His followers to do?

What implications do His commands have on us?

How would you assess your willingness to obey His commands as defining markers of your membership in the kingdom of God?

Chapter 3

HOPE AND THE COMMUNITY OF JESUS

After this the Lord appointed seventy-two others and sent them two by two ahead of him to every town and place where he was about to go.

—Luke 10:1

Jesus sent teams into the harvest. teams of two. Teams were sent in addition to the original twelve disciples. But why teams? Why two by two? He could have sent His followers to seventy-two locations but narrowed His scope in half and only sent them to thirty-six places in teams of two.

Charles Swindoll recalls his training in the United States Marine Corps when reflecting on this verse. He says, "We were taught in the Marines that when you dig a foxhole before a battle, always dig it big enough for two men. Two men fighting in the trenches strengthen and encourage each other. They maintain level heads. They are more effective in fighting and have a much better chance for survival. On the other hand, one warrior in combat can easily become discouraged and retreat from the fight. In pairs, soldiers enjoy the benefits of companionship, protection, affirmation, and encouragement."[37] Ministry, while not the same as military service

---

[37] Charles Swindoll, *Insights on Luke* (Colorado Springs: NavPress, 2017), PDF ebook.

and battle, is not very easy. It has its own set of challenges and crises. Throughout the Bible there are many examples of pairs. In the Old Testament pairs occur such as Moses and Aaron, Joshua and Caleb, and Naomi and Ruth, but this was not the normal pattern of the day.[38] In the New Testament we find James and John, Paul and Barnabas, and Paul and Timothy. Jesus established a universal pattern of pairs or teams in the sending of missionaries in this passage that became a precedent in early Christianity.[39]

I recall vividly the scenes on television of the outbreak of the Muslim Brotherhood Revolution in January 2011. Crowds flooded the National Museum Plaza in Cairo, Egypt, to protest, set fires, and form mobs to raise their voices against political conditions. The Arab Spring was underway, followed by President Hosni Mubarak's overthrow a month later. It was a dangerous time and an unsafe place to be. One year prior, I led a group of pastors to visit Buckner ministry in Cairo. Buckner was in collaboration with a local NGO (non-governmental organization), providing services to Muslim families through a Family Hope Center. We visited historic sites, including the pyramids, floated down the Nile River, and visited ministry sites in that city. We enjoyed placing shoes on children's feet at a children's home, serving families at the Family Hope Center, and visiting incredibly beautiful sites. We rode camels and practiced conversational Arabic. We found lots of commonality between Hispanic and Arab culture, language, and history.

And as I sat watching the television set, I could not believe my eyes, as I witnessed the destruction in the National Museum Plaza, the protests and the violence erupting in places I had walked with these pastors just a few months earlier. While on that trip, I assigned

---

[38] James R. Edwards, *The Gospel according to Luke* (Grand Rapids: William B. Eerdmans Publishing Company, 2015), 305.
[39] Ibid.

the group in teams of two. It was the buddy system. I felt that was the best way to keep track of the group. The buddy system was not only set up for protection and safety but also for fellowship, encouragement, and companionship. One member of our group was sort of a "free-spirit" and sometimes wandered aimlessly. The buddy system ensured we knew were he was and kept him safe.

Benefits of Teams of Two

There clearly are benefits to the commissioned followers of Jesus to have been sent in teams of two. Benefits like courage, companionship,[40] confirmation of what would take place by another witness, and safety.[41] Perhaps the greatest benefit to teams of two is a sense of community. In the beginning when God created Adam, He said it is not good for man be alone. No creature in all creation was able to provide Adam with companionship and a sense of community. God knew Adam needed a companion, a helper. He created Eve from Adam (Genesis 2:18–25). Adam and Eve were the first team, the first two-by-two team in all creation. Yet, this is not the first example of community in the biblical record.

When the biblical writer recorded the first sentences of human history, God said, "Let us make mankind in our image, in our likeness" (Genesis 1:26). In God, the Creator, is expressed a plurality of persons. I mentioned in chapter two that Jesus was with God and was God in the very beginning of time as recorded in John's Gospel (John 1:1). The Apostle Paul also picked up this theme in his letter to the Colossians when speaking of Jesus. He wrote, "The Son is the image of the invisible God, the firstborn over all creation. For by Him

---

[40] Herschel H. Hobbs, *An Exposition of the Gospel of Luke* (Grand Rapids: Baker Book House, 1966), 178.

[41] Richard B. Vinson, Luke: Volume 21 of Smyth and Helwys Bible Commentary (Macon, GA: Smyth & Helwys, 2008), 320.

all things were created: things in heaven and on earth, visible and invisible" (Colossians 1:15–17). The first example of community in biblical history is in the person of God, the Creator, with Jesus and the Spirit of God, the third person of this community (Genesis 1:2). In the beginning there was one God in three persons: Father, Son, and Spirit.

George Cladis paints a picture of this image of God as a choreography, a circle dance of the Father, the Son, and the Holy Spirit. He described the circle dance of God as full of joy, freedom, song, intimacy, and harmony.[42] It is a picture of community. The definition of community can be broken into two words: common and unity. There is a sense of commonality and unity in the three persons of God. Their commonality is about harmony in purpose, direction, and mission. God is three persons with the same purpose and mission in redemptive history. Their unity is expressed in a single focus and desire for humanity. People need community too. We need each other. We are not whole without other people in our lives. We need people like family, friends, colleagues, and neighbors in our lives. We live in society and were made to enjoy relationships. In those relationships and circles, we can find support, community, and hope for the most difficult moments in life. The basis of our hope is found in the community of the redeemed, a redeemed community on mission and life in the community of the King. But I don't think just any ordinary community will do. Humanity and community left to itself does not always produce a positive and healthy environment where people are offered dignity, respect, acceptance, love, forgiveness, healing, support, and encouragement. What kind of community satisfies the deepest needs of our souls? The community of the redeemed provides the kind of community

---

[42] George Cladis, *Leading the Team-Based Church: How Pastors and Church Staffs Can Grow Together into a Powerful Fellowship of Leaders* (San Francisco: Jossey-Bass, 1999), 4.

that is good in and of itself. It is the kind of community we need as humans. It is the kind of community we long and hope for in this life.

Community of the Redeemed

The community of the redeemed is a group of two or more people who know they are sinners. They know they have been called out of a life of darkness into a life of light. They know they are sinners who need a Savior, a Redeemer. They know that without a savior they can never really know who they are; they can never really know their purpose for living; they may not ever experience the depth of forgiveness, restoration, acceptance, and love modeled for us in the person of Jesus Christ. In the community of the redeemed, you know you are loved. You know your Creator values you. You know you are accepted despite your sins, your flaws, and your imperfections. You know you have grace and mercy for the times when you fail. You know in the community of the redeemed you get what you don't deserve, and you don't get what you do deserve. Rather than calling the kingdom a place to call home, the kingdom is really a relationship with the kingdom, a kingship.[43] It is a relationship with Jesus the King where you find peace and hope. A key to this kind of community and to membership in the kingdom is the quality of the relationship with the King. Love is at the heart of the good life. A love for God and a love for our neighbors are linked.[44] This loving quality of relationships in the community of the redeemed, in the kingdom, is a witness to the world that we are disciples of Jesus.[45] Do you have a circle of friends like this? A community of the redeemed can be created with one or two other people whose lives have been transformed by the Redeemer.

---

[43] Cook, *Living in the Kingdom*, 18.

[44] Ibid., 32–34.

[45] Ibid., 42.

The community of the redeemed is where Jesus, the Redeemer, comes near. He is also the glue that holds the community together. He said, "For where two or three are gathered in my name, there am I with them" (Matthew 18:20). Jesus gathers redeemed people who have been called out of darkness into the light. These folks are formed into churches. The word for church in New Testament Greek is *eklesia,* coming from two Greek words: *ek* meaning "out of" and *klesia,* from *kaleo,* meaning "called." The church is the "called out" people—called out from darkness into the light. The main idea of the church is this: "the people of God redeemed or called out for a special purpose. The focus is on living in reality, not a building, an organization, or a place . . . God is calling out a new covenant people to further his redemptive purposes throughout the world."[46]

This new covenant people cuts across cultures, gender, geography, political affiliation, and language. The church in this sense is universal and global, made up of people from every tribe, nation, culture, and language (Revelation 7:9). Wherever and whenever the "called out" come together under the banner of Jesus the King, we find "community and fellowship was essentially a power at work, in the present, exercising its force. It also concerned a community, a house, an area 'where the goods of salvation are available and received.'"[47] The church, which is the community of the redeemed, the called-out people, is where we find genuine, authentic relationships focused on a special mission with special purpose. This is the good life, also called kingdom living.[48] This sense of community is the new people of God versus our previous condition of being alone, alienated, separated, and apart from God and each other due to the negative

---

[46] Boyd Hunt, *Redeemed! Eschatological Redemption and the Kingdom of God.* (Nashville: Baptist Sunday School Board, 1993), 173.

[47] Glasser, et al., *Announcing the Kingdom,* 186.

[48] Cook, *Living in the Kingdom,* 6.

impact of sin. We no longer live for ourselves, but in Christ we live for each other, serving one another, on mission in the world.

New People—Pueblo Nuevo

In 1992 my wife Belinda and I moved from Dallas to El Paso, Texas, to start a new church as part of Scotsdale Baptist Church in that city. Belinda resigned from a tenure-track position as assistant professor of communication disorders at Texas Christian University, and I resigned from my first full-time pastorate at North Temple Baptist Church across from Dallas Love Field Airport. We were young and full of energy and hope. We were on mission to establish a new community of the redeemed. One of the most thrilling experiences was gathering with a group of Jesus followers already in El Paso to start this church. They were members of other El Paso area churches. They gave of their own resources and time to form a new community of the redeemed. We focused on sharing the good news with other people not yet in the community of faith. We developed relationships and friendships and invited people from our collective circles of influence to Bible study and worship. We invited people to receive and share unconditional love, grace, mercy, salvation, fellowship, forgiveness, and purpose with a sense of mission to reach others.

We saw ourselves as a new people, a new community of faith. We saw people in our circle of influence become part of this new community. We named the church Pueblo Nuevo Community Church. This name means "new people." We grew from five families to a congregation of about 120, and we started several new churches that also started new churches. Church planting proved to be the most challenging and rewarding ministry my wife and I ever attempted. Twenty-five years later, those churches are still serving communities in the El Paso area. We grew as a community of faith, and we also grew lifelong friendships.

This new community became a place where faith was found. Neighbors became friends, and friends became family. We shared our lives. We started our families together, raised our children together, and bore each other's burdens. We prayed together and for each other. We prayed over each other's children. We grew to love each other. Everyone who came into this community was accepted. We found acceptance, forgiveness, restoration, and redemption in a place we could call home. We were guided by the Spirit of God and the story of His Word in Scripture. We introduced friends to a relationship with Jesus. They grew in relationship to Him. They learned the way of Jesus and grew spiritually, introducing others to the possibility of Jesus in their lives. We found peace in tough times. The Lord held us together in times of loss, grief, and conflict. We learned to find hope in this community because Jesus was at work in our lives. He was present. He was near.

Community in Mission

Over the course of serving as a vocational pastor and minister, I have found community while on task, on mission as a servant. In fact, most of the closest friends I have today came out of serving in ministry, on mission. Followers of Jesus in teams of two would also find community, companionship, and camaraderie while on mission for Jesus. This is true for followers of Jesus today. When you are on mission, serving the King, a sense of community will be a benefit of obedience and service. Blessing flows out of obedience on mission. Serving together on mission and in teams to bring hope, peace, healing, and justice to the lives of others also provides many blessings and benefits.

There are five clear benefits of working as a team on mission.[49] The church, organized in ministry teams or church-planting teams,

---

[49] David W. Shenk and Ervin Stutzman, *Creating Communities of the Kingdom: New Testament Models of Church Planting* (Scottsdale, PA: Herald Press, 1988), 44.

models for others what it means to live and work together in repentance and harmony. I am not a perfect individual, and neither were the people who I have worked with. In the context of working with each other, we inevitably offend each other and become alienated from each other. Hurt feelings, misunderstandings, miscommunication, and unintended offenses are common. So what do we do when that happens? We tap the resources of grace and forgiveness that enable us to repair and restore what was damaged. This process in turn deepens our relationships when done correctly according to biblical patterns. This process is lived out in public in the full view of others who may have never seen repentance, forgiveness, and restoration of relationships in action. We experienced this restoration on a regular basis.

Another benefit of serving as a team on mission is the potential for diversity across cultures. At Pueblo Nuevo we had both Euro-American and Hispanic-American members and leaders. Among the Hispanic members, we had members of native Texan backgrounds as well as Puerto Rican background. We had multigenerational borderlanders (native to the El Paso, Texas—Juarez, Mexico, borderlands) and newcomers from South Texas. We designed that church to connect both Anglo and Hispanic friends in El Paso who were primarily professionals from that area. We saw this diversity as an advantage over being a monocultural church with relational circles in one culture.

A third benefit of working in teams on mission is the opportunity to share power in the leadership. Authority and leadership can be diffused among members and leaders. At Pueblo Nuevo everybody worked and contributed in one way or another. Leadership was something everybody participated in, and the work was distributed. Power was shared. We had Bible study group leaders, worship leaders, children's ministry leaders, greeters, logistics teams, and the list goes on.

A fourth benefit of working in teams on mission is the advantage of assisting each other in the work itself. More teams means more people with skills, abilities, and resources for the mission. Teams allow individual gifts and contributions to be made for the mission. At Pueblo Nuevo we tried to figure out the giftedness of our members and then assigned them to teams where those gifts were needed, which advanced our mission.

The fifth benefit of working in teams on mission is the synergy that is created. Pharmacists are aware of the simultaneous action of separate chemicals and the greater effect those chemicals have when working together as opposed to individual ingredients working alone.[50] The same is true on a team. The sum of the whole is greater than the parts working in harmony. Synergy is also contagious. It is the sense of togetherness and community found when working in a team on mission. The quality of life and relationships as governed by the King who calls us to action creates a unique experience in living. At Pueblo Nuevo we experienced a unique chemistry of leaders, giftings, and cultures. This sense of community was attractive to other people we encountered. The fellowship was deep and rich. The relationships and friendships were of great value. We were able to do together what we would never have been able to do alone. I recall one event that drew about seven hundred people in a community we were connecting with. We served a meal and provided music, face painting, and games for children, blood-pressure screenings, and hair styling for women. We had nurses, hair stylists, musicians, and teens willing to serve. A team of about forty-five people came together to hold a community event that far exceeded our expectations. We distributed Bibles and formed a few Bible studies, creating the foundation for a new church. There is no way any of us could have

---

[50] Ibid., 49.

done this alone. Working together as a team produced a high level of synergy and incredible results for the kingdom.

Life in the Community of the King

Two or three people who come together in the name of Jesus of Nazareth, called for a specific purpose on mission for the King, produce a unique way of living. It is living life in the community of the King. When the King comes near and becomes our King, we submit our lives under His authority and rule. We want what He wants. We want to do what He does. We want to imitate Him. We want to act like Him. We want to live by His rules. We want to please Him. He is our resurrected King who gave His life as a ransom for us. How can we live in any other way? Thom Wolf raised the question: What is the best way to live life on the planet? My answer is plain and simple. It is the Jesus way. It is Jesus who showed us how to live and how to treat others the way we want to be treated. Jesus showed us how to love those difficult to love. He also showed us how to respect women and to value cultures different from our own. Jesus showed us how to offer grace and mercy and how to forgive the person who offended us. He demonstrated compassion for the crowds, healing for the sick, and food for the hungry. He taught that we should love our enemies and bless those who persecute us. He provided an ethic that has stood the test of time.

Buckner International is a faith-based organization. Another way of saying it is we pattern all our work with clients, staff, trustees, and donors after the pattern of Jesus of Nazareth. While we are not perfect, the Jesus way is clearly our aspiration and sense of organizational values and culture. Who we are, how we live, how we work, and how we relate to each other is what we have to offer. We offer life in the community of the King. We offer this life to each other, our clients, our friends, and our donors. This is the sweet fragrance of our ministry. The Jesus way has become the Buckner way, patterned after our founder. We offer the possibility of hope to the child who has been abandoned, neglected, and abused. We offer hope to the single mom who has suffered domestic violence or economic difficulty and for her children who live in fear. We offer hope to the family in turmoil on the edge of disintegration. We offer a sense of hope and dignity for the senior at the sunset of life. Hope is a possibility in the community of the King. When hope shines brightly, people sense peace is near. How does peace become a possibility for people in pain, turmoil, loss, and discouragement? How can we access that sense of peace amid the storm?

Questions to Consider

Have you ever been on a team (in sports, in business, in the military)?

What did you learn from being on a team of two or more?

What is community, and how important is it to you?

What does living in community of the redeemed, of the kingdom, mean to you?

Over the course of your experience with Christ, what are the relationships you have now that you may not have ever enjoyed before knowing Jesus as your King?

Chapter 4

HOPE AND THE POSSIBILITY OF PEACE

When you enter a house, first say, "Peace to this house." If someone who promotes peace is there, your peace will rest on him; if not, it will return to you. Stay there, eating and drinking whatever they give you, for the worker deserves his wages. Do not move around from house to house.

—Luke 10:5–7

Peace is not the absence of turmoil. When peace comes, problems may persist. Peace is not the absence of illness, pain, or difficulty. Peace is the calm assurance in the middle of the storm. Peace comes when it makes no sense to be calm. Peace is the overwhelming assurance that everything is going to be OK in the middle of chaos. Would you welcome this kind of peace? Have you ever needed peace in chaotic moments?

Marissa needed peace. She struggled with bipolar disorder and depression. Her mood swings created havoc in her home. She struggled with anger issues coupled with alcohol abuse. She dropped out of school at age fifteen. Scars inflicted by her own hand ran up and down her left forearm. One unhealthy lifestyle decision led to another, including a five-year unhealthy relationship and a child named Addisyn. Marissa and Addisyn lived in Longview, Texas. They shared a small bed. They accessed warm water through a small water heater and boiled water on most days to meet their needs. They lived in a recreational vehicle supported by Marissa's job as a cashier at a nearby gas station. This is not what Marissa had in mind for her daughter. Marissa did not have access to higher education and did not have a driver's license. Fear gripped Marissa: fear of failure, fear of the unknown. Marissa needed peace and hope not just for her but for her daughter Addy.[51] Where could Marissa find peace and hope for the future? Where could she turn for help? Who would step in to make a difference in her life situation?

Last year at a shoe distribution at Burnett Elementary in Dallas, I recall standing in the lobby of the school greeting hundreds of parents who came to the event. The school lobby was noisy, busy, and bustling with excitement and joy. I joined Buckner staff and Principal Sonya Loskot and her staff to serve the families whose children were enrolled in her school. We had games and educational seminars and distributed food and shoes. This was one of the first events we held in the community to announce we were introducing a new Buckner Family Hope Center in that area. We had leaflets printed with a sample drawing of the new building and a listing of services we planned to offer, including English as a second language, computer skills, parenting skills, after-school programs, job skills training, financial education, and other services to strengthen families.

A lady approached me with the flier in her hand and said, "Excuse me, can you tell me what this is all about?" I answered her with a general explanation of what Buckner was doing in the area. Then she raised the Buckner leaflet and said, "I know where this property is, but I can't find the building. Where is it?" I said, "Oh, I am so sorry, this is a future building. We are about

---

[51] Adapted from John Hall, "A Visible Change," Buckner International, April 16, 2018, https://www.buckner.org/article/a-visible-change/.

two years away from opening since we first have to raise funds and then build." The look on her face conveyed a feeling of despair and disappointment. She said, "But I need these services now." I did not know what to say. All I could think was to tell her, "Someday we will have those services ready for the public, but we are a few years away from that."[52] Her family had deep needs. She was hopeful, but I could not help her that day. She lacked peace; she needed hope. I could not give it to her that day. My heart sank.

Lorena was in a difficult situation. She needed to leave her home and take her two sons with her. Her husband was a drug addict. She knew she had to leave for the welfare of her children. She lacked the skills to work at a job that could support her family. She had nowhere to go and no money. She landed in a hotel and began working there for three years. The family was crammed into one room with no kitchen.[53] She needed hope in a hopeless situation; she needed peace in a chaotic situation. Where would she go? What would she do? Who would she turn to?

Rhoda is a sixty-two-year-old grandmother living in Kitale, Kenya. She is a mother of ten and has suffered the loss of four of her children. She is also a grandmother of nineteen children. Her first husband died in 1972. She had few options to survive with six children, so she remarried but was thrown out of her home by her in-laws in 2008. She resorted to part-time work to provide for her family and in 2012 was diagnosed with cervical cancer. She was at her wit's end. She had few options for survival with overwhelming odds against her.[54] She had no peace. She had no hope. She had

---

[52] Albert Reyes, "Perspectives on Buckner," *Buckner Today*, Summer 2018, 4.

[53] Adapted from John Hall, "Family Pathways: Transforming vulnerable families," *Buckner Today*, Summer 2018, 18.

[54] Adapted from Scott Collins, "Family Ties: Buckner Kenya Ministries Strengthen Families to Protect Children," *Buckner Today*, Summer 2018, 26.

nobody to turn to. How would she survive? How would she provide? Where would she turn?

Peace to This House: Meaning in the First Century

Marissa, Lorena, and Rhoda represent households that need peace and hope. We approached their homes and families with the same assignment and task Jesus gave to the teams He sent out. Jesus said, "When you enter a house, first say, 'Peace to this house.'" Our task is no different today, but what did it mean in the first century?

The phrase, "Peace to this house," is a blessing that renders the meaning of the Hebrew word *shalom*. It goes deeper than the absence of war or battles or arguments. Rather, it carries with it the idea of well-being, health,[55] wholeness, and prosperity in every aspect of life. For the Jew, *shalom* carried the meaning of the quality of life promised in the kingdom of God.[56] Peace carried with it a sense of God's goodwill toward those in the home and all that salvation would bring.[57] The greeting of peace is also a promise of blessings of the kingdom.[58] The greeting of peace brought with it the promise of fullness of life, dynamic and concrete relationships, and the sign of the messianic kingdom.[59] The disciples were announcing the kingdom of Jesus coming. This kingdom was coming to private homes and cities.

When entering a home in the first century it was customary to give a greeting, and the kind of greeting Jesus instructs was also

---

[55] Richard Blight, *An Exegetical Summary of Luke 1–11* (Dallas: SIL International, 2008), 451.

[56] Swindoll, *Insights on Luke*, PDF ebook.

[57] Edwards, *The Gospel according to Luke*, 307.

[58] Vinson, Luke: Volume 21 of Smyth and Helwys Bible Commentary, 324.

[59] François Bovon, *Luke 2: A Commentary on the Gospel of Luke 9:51–19:27* (Minneapolis: Fortress Press, 2013), 28.

a normal greeting. However, when Jesus gave this greeting in the context of sending out teams to new homes and cities, it is associated with the coming of the salvation of God.[60] The disciples brought good news wherever they went. They were peacemakers. The whole scope of their work could be summed up as proclaiming and bringing peace with God, with themselves, with all others, and with all circumstances.[61] This was good news in a chaotic and politically charged first century. How relevant was the notion of peace in the first century? Would this have resonated with those who heard the greeting in their homes? Did it matter to them?

Peace in the First Century

What did peace look like in the first century? To understand the difference the Christian concept of peace made, one must first understand the context in which the Christian faith emerged. Christianity was born in the basin of the Mediterranean Sea in the first century. Roman rule and instability was the order of the day. Pax Romana made for the spread of ideas with the building of roads and the growth of commerce in that region. Greek and Latin were the two languages spoken in that region. A period of social insecurity grew as individuals were uprooted from their environments as slaves, soldiers, or by free choice. Many found themselves unsupported by the social group in which they had been reared. Individuals were absorbed into growing cities and a burgeoning empire as impersonal citizens and subjects. Millions were disinherited and deracinated. Slaves were transported to all parts of the empire and landed on estates and in cities foreign to them. People were hungry for a moral

---

[60] I. Howard Marshall, *The Gospel of Luke: A Commentary on the Greek Text* (Grand Rapids: William B. Eerdmans Publishing Company, 1978), 419.

[61] Alexander Maclaren, *Expositions of Holy Scripture: St. Luke* (Grand Rapids: Baker Book House, 1978), 312.

compass and a sense of self-respect. The average citizen sought sustaining relationships and a sense of community. As cities grew, they were increasingly made up of many strangers, their children, and newcomers from distant lands and other parts of the Roman Empire. At the close of the second century, disasters began to strike the Roman Empire bringing on a period of social disintegration. The Roman government tried to solve problems, but confidence in the government to make sense out of life waned. A growing "loss of nerve" was prevalent among the vast Graeco-Roman population.[62]

Living in cities in the first century in the Graeco-Roman world was a challenging experience. Rodney Stark has noted that extraordinary levels of urban disorder including filth, disease, social dislocation, misery, fear, and cultural chaos characterized first century cities, which were small but densely populated. Antioch, for example, had 75,000 inhabitants, or about 117 people per acre versus cities today like Chicago, San Francisco, and New York City that have 21, 23, and 37 people living per acre of land.[63] Cities were very crowded. Limited water supply, inadequate sewage disposal, outdoor cooking, and mixed living quarters with livestock made for extremely challenging conditions for citizens.

A widespread preoccupation with sexual activity was prevalent. Homosexuality was common in Greek society, and prostitution was a normal and expected occurrence. Children suffered a high mortality rate and were considered valuable for the security of the community and of their parents. Life expectancy for women was shorter than for men. Most families only had one child. Families of four and five were very rare. Girls were considered a liability due to the requirement to pay a dowry at marriage. The answer

[62] Kenneth Scott Latourette, *A History of Christianity, Volume 1: Beginnings to 1500* (San Francisco: Harper San Francisco, 1953), 22–23.
[63] Stark, *The Rise of Christianity*, 149.

to overpopulation was infanticide. Abortions were the order of the day, often taking the life of the mother as well. The economy was primarily agricultural in most cities with no major industrial opportunities. The marketplace was the center of the city's activity. The poor were paid low wages with little opportunity for economic growth or advancement.[64]

It is clear life in Graeco-Roman society was challenging at best. The living conditions in cities, the welfare of children, the widespread moral decay, the lack of community and social connections, and the sense of widespread despair and economic oppression created an environment in which peace, as described earlier, was not common. Stark argues that once Christianity appeared, "its superior capacity for meeting chronic problems became evident to all. Since Antioch, for example, suffered from these chronic problems, it needed solutions. It is no wonder Christian missionaries were welcomed when they arrived there. Stark contends that Christians made life more tolerable in Graeco-Roman cities.[65] Christians who offered peace as the first order of business in new relationships brought a fresh, new perspective and a new way of life.

Peace in the Twenty-First Century

I used to think that living in the twenty-first century meant we have experienced much progress in the human condition, in society, in technology, and in educational and social advancement. We have seen many advances across all sectors of society. However, as I take time to consider how we have advanced as a society in terms of moral and wholesome living, I am not so convinced we are getting any better here in the United States of America. In fact, it seems

---

[64] Everett Ferguson, *Backgrounds of Early Christianity*, Third Edition (Grand Rapids: William B. Eerdmanns Publishing Company, 2003).

[65] Stark, *The Rise of Christianity*, 162.

we are sliding backwards in many ways. While we are advancing economically, many are still left out of an opportunity to work and prosper. We may be one of the richest countries in the world, but we also suffer from a growing number of suicides, human trafficking, abortions, divorce, family disintegration, and a general sense of despair. We are fragmented politically and seem to have lost our way from civility to increasing levels of hostility and shameful behavior displayed in public and in the media, especially in social media. Drug abuse, alcoholism, domestic violence, sexual abuse, child abuse, mass shootings, and a meltdown of the family unit seem to have reached epidemic proportions. These issues represent the new normal. The increasing number of children removed from their families and placed in foster care seems to skyrocket where economic activity is booming. People live without meaning, purpose, or a sense of direction. We might be advanced technologically and a prosperous society, but do we have peace? When life does not turn out the way we planned, where do we go to get help, to find hope?

How Do Hope and Peace Work Together?

Peace comes to us when the Prince of Peace lives in us. Even in the most dreadful and unexpected situations, we can find peace. We have access to the peace that passes all understanding (Philippians 4:7). In other words, this kind of peace makes no sense from a human point of view. When you should be frazzled, a nervous wreck, discouraged, and at your lowest point in life, you can find peace, peace that only Jesus brings to you. The follower of Jesus filled with His Spirit is given peace as a fruit of Christ dwelling in us (Galatians 5:22). The Apostle Paul encouraged us to allow the peace of Christ to dwell richly in us (Colossians 3:15). We have the real possibility of peace in moments of great challenge and pain. The possibility of peace gives hope. The reality of peace provides hope. I have hope because

I know Jesus is with me and provides what I need regardless of the situation.

Marissa first found her way to peace when she entered a Buckner program called Project HOPES, a program designed to help parents with skills for successful parenting. She set goals to obtain a driver's license. Next, she participated in family coaching at the Buckner Family Hope Center in Longview. She entered a Jobs for Life class and successfully completed that program. She was ready for the next step and qualified for the Buckner Family Pathways program to live in an apartment and begin her education toward an associate of arts degree. The program staff taught her how to balance life as a mother and a student. She learned how to be independent. Marissa's daughter Addy was enrolled in an excellent preschool program and bonded with her mother; both thrived in a place of peace and hope. Despite the incredible obstacles she faced, she found peace. Over time she began to hope again. Her goals and her plans for her family began to materialize.

Lorena found her way to the Buckner Family Pathways program in Amarillo, Texas. She found a place of security and peace for her and her two sons. They are in a safe environment away from potential abuse. She has enrolled in an associate of arts degree program in Amarillo and is on her way to restart her family in a new life toward financial independence. She found peace. Now, she has hope for a bright future.

Rhoda found peace too. She participated in the Buckner Family Hope Center in Kitale, Kenya. She learned how to make bread and began her own bakery. She realized she enjoyed baking bread and turned that strength into a way to provide for her family. She took the earnings from her bakery business and bought seventeen chickens, twenty-five chicks, two sheep, and two rabbits. She learned skills through economic empowerment that have totally changed her life. She found peace. Then she began to hope for a brighter future.

"Peace to this house" means goodwill and wholeness. It means dynamic and concrete relationships, and blessings that come with the kingdom of Jesus. Peace was what Marissa, Lorena, and Rhoda needed first and foremost. Once peace was a possibility, hope followed. Peace and hope are essential. What about healing?

Questions to Consider

What did the concept of peace mean in the first century?

What does peace mean today?

What does peace look like in your life?

Why is peace so essential?

How do peace and hope work together in your circle of influence?

Chapter 5

HOPE AND PEACE AS HEALING

When you enter a town and are welcomed, eat what is offered to you. Heal the sick who are there and tell them, "The kingdom of God has come near to you."

—Luke 10:8–9

Imagine a life in which there is no healing. You break your arm or suffer a deep wound, but no help is on the way. Recovery does not exist. There is no help, no hope. You live with the damage, with the loss, and with the hurt. Your body tries to heal itself to no avail. You have a scar, a deformed arm, or even worse, abscess or infection invades your body. This is your new life after a physical loss. No healing, no hope, and no peace. What about emotional losses?

Imagine a life in which there is no healing for emotional scars, abuse, depression, discouragement, or relational conflict. Imagine the loss from economic hardship, mistakes, or failures in the marketplace. There is no healing, no recovery. This is your new life. You just learn to adjust and live with loss, with less, with pain.

Now imagine just for a moment that healing is possible in this life. Imagine that it could be possible in an instant. How would you feel about that possibility? What would you do if you heard all you had to do was get close enough to a person that could heal you? You don't need an appointment. You don't need to know somebody who can introduce you. You don't even need to have a conversation. All you must do is get close enough to touch that person to be healed. What if you learned His name was Jesus of Nazareth?

One woman did exactly that. She suffered from a bleeding disorder for twelve years. Twelve years of loss, pain, embarrassment, and shame. She heard that healing could happen instantly just by touching Jesus' garment. She had enough information and a determination to get close enough to Jesus to touch Him. As Jesus walked through her town, people surrounded Him. I imagine shoving and pushing to the point of danger. She would have to be determined to brave the crowd, to make her way toward Jesus. She might have to push, shove, and weave her way through the crowd to get close enough to reach Him. So with the crowds almost crushing Jesus as He walked through the town, she came up behind Him and touched the edge of His cloak, and immediately her bleeding stopped. Jesus felt it and said, "Who touched me?" His disciples were aghast. The crowd was so big and pressing against Him, how could He identify a single touch, much less, identify the person who touched Him? The question seemed a bit ridiculous to the disciples, impossible to answer.

But Jesus insisted and said, "Someone touched me; I know that power has gone out from me." Jesus could sense the power that went from Him to heal the woman. The woman knew she could not go unnoticed, so she came forward and fell at the feet of Jesus and began to tremble. She told everyone about her situation and how she had been healed on the spot. Jesus said "Daughter, your faith has healed you. Go in peace" (Luke 8:43–48). This scenario is hard to imagine, but it really did happen. In fact, sick people found healing simply by touching Jesus' cloak so often that word began to spread. People began begging for the opportunity to get close enough to Jesus to touch his cloak for instant healing (Matthew 14:36).

There are numerous examples in the Gospels that demonstrate how Jesus healed people with physical issues. Jairus, a synagogue leader, knew his daughter was dying, or so he thought. Jairus thought he could reach Jesus in time to heal his daughter, but it was too late. "Your daughter is dead. Don't bother the teacher anymore," one of Jairus's servants said. Jesus heard this conversation and said, "Don't be afraid; just believe, and she will be healed." When Jesus arrived at his house, Jairus did not allow anyone to go into the house except Jesus, Peter, John, and James with the child's mother and himself. Jesus said, "She is not dead but asleep." So, Jesus took her by the hand and said, "My child, get up!" Her spirit returned, and she stood up at once. Her parents were astonished" (Luke 8:49–56).

Most of the healing experiences in the Gospels happened just this way, immediately. But not all healing by Jesus was resolved immediately. In fact, when He sent His disciples out and told them to heal the sick (Luke 9:1–6), He was not expecting an immediate resolution. The disciples would have to arrive, engage, and begin a process of healing among the people they encountered. The first step is to arrive, to show up, to come near to those we wish to serve.

Ashlee was reeling from what felt like a series of failures and the death of her best friend; she was a shell of her former self. She woke each morning in a pit of pain, reliving hard moments in her life. She believed she deserved this. She was unworthy of joy or pleasure. She had no peace, just pain. She had no hope, just loss. When she finally realized her lifestyle prevented her from being the kind of mom she wanted to be, she found herself in the Buckner Family Pathways program in Conroe, Texas. This ministry provides housing, counseling, and assistance for single-parent families, so parents can accomplish their educational goals and strengthen their families. Ashlee told her counselors, "When I came here, I had lost faith in the journey God had for me. I had lost faith in myself. I felt like I had failed in so many things. I felt like I failed at completing my education. I was now a single mom. I felt like I had started a lot of things and had not finished them." After an initial conversation with two Buckner staff members, they and Ashlee bowed their heads in prayer. Ashlee doesn't remember the exact words voiced but remembers what happened when the two Buckner staff showed up to listen to her story and then prayed for her.

"I felt like in that moment, God sent down angels on me when I said 'Yes, I'll work with you and trust God,'" she said. "It was like a complete change. I looked like a different person. I felt like a different person. I believed. My thought process changed. Everything changed." Ashlee went through grief counseling and a class on prayer. Through prayer, texts, and conversations, Anna Rodriquez and Carrie Johnson, both Buckner staff, have encouraged her along the way.

Ashlee said, "Anna and Carrie help my child and me see ourselves in a way God would like to see us. They see us as who we are becoming, not as we are right now. They don't see us as a broken vase trying to get put back together. They see the fully completed vase and treat us like that every single day. It's awesome to have somebody treat you like a crystal vase when you feel like shattered pieces on the floor."

Today, Ashlee is a different person. Her faith grew, as did her determination. Her eyes are bright, her voice full of energy. She's put her past behind her and is forging a bright future—one goal at a time. "Everything they're offering is for me to grow," she said. "I can say, 'Ashlee, how far do you want to go? Do you want to go the next step?'" Ashlee is determined to keep saying yes, believing if God is on her side, there are no limits. She sees more possibilities for her life. Her confidence grows as she accomplishes what she previously thought impossible. She has become a leader among the moms in the

Family Pathways program. Ashlee is enrolled at Lone Star College in Conroe, where she'll earn her associate's degree then begin working on her bachelor's degree and later a master's degree. She wants to be a teacher so she can help shape young minds. The first step on this journey was incarnational. Anna and Carrie showed up in Ashlee's life. They came to listen and pray. Everything changed after that.

Hope, Peace, and Healing Are Incarnational

Jesus said, "When you enter a town and are welcomed" (Luke 10:8). The first step may sound too simple. They must arrive. They must show up first. I have come to realize that for most things in life, including ministry, you must show up. It is not more complicated than what Jesus did as recorded in John 1:14. John says the Word became flesh. The Word became incarnational. Jesus showed up. He broke into human history in a town called Bethlehem. That is precisely what these disciples were to do. They were to enter a town. They were to show up. They were to arrive and hope for a warm welcome. They were to be received by those they went to visit. Their arrival resembled a triumphal entrance into the city with food to follow.[66]

Early in my tenure with Buckner International, I accompanied a friend and colleague, Dr. Abraham Sarkar, to a village near Dhaka, Bangladesh. We were there to visit small towns and villages and demonstrate the love of Jesus through economic development activities. A big part of the trip was just getting there and showing up. We flew to Dhaka and then took a bus to outlying villages in agricultural areas. I will never forget arriving near the village where buses and cars could not pass through due to a lack of passable roads. We were then transferred to rickshaws driven by a young man on a

---

[66] F. Godet, *A Commentary on the Gospel of St. Luke* (New York: I. K. Funk & Co., 1881), 295.

bicycle. We traveled for a mile or two and came to the place where we would disembark the rickshaw. Next, we began to walk toward the village center. To my amazement, the whole village seemed to welcome us. Several hundred children met us and cheered on our arrival. The welcome line was about two hundred yards long. The children broke into a welcome song and placed flowered wreaths around our necks. I finally arrived at the place where village leaders welcomed us formally. Flowers were thrown into the air, and words of welcome were given. Wow! We arrived and were generously welcomed with joy, smiles, laughter, and singing. None of this would have been possible had we not shown up. Hope, peace, and healing begin with us showing up.

Hope, Peace, and Healing Are Engaging

Jesus said, "When you enter a town and are welcomed, eat what is offered to you" (Luke 10:8). Showing up is the first step. What follows is to engage with the people you meet. There is nothing quite like sharing a meal. The disciples were to eat whatever was offered. To refuse the food offered would be rude and disrespectful. However, to eat what was offered would convey honor to the hosts. To share the meal at a table is to share time, conversation, and presence. I know what it is like to sit at the table of someone who has welcomed you into their home or city. Having traveled to over twenty countries in North, Central, and South America, Europe, Southeast Asia, and Africa, I have shared meals in a wide variety of places. The food has always been good even though I was not always sure what I was eating, and the fellowship has always been rich. I have shared meals with very poor families and very wealthy ones. I have had the privilege of sharing meals with people with no power or authority, and I have enjoyed meals with people at the highest levels of government. In each situation the meal at the table or the coffee time is a powerful way of engaging with them.

Engaging new friends while sharing a meal provides opportunities for conversation and for getting to know one another. Showing up and engaging new friends opens the door for healing. Hope, peace, and healing begin with engaging people you meet.

Hope, Peace, and Healing Are a Process

Jesus said, "Heal the sick who are there and tell them, 'The kingdom of God has come near to you'" (Luke 10:9). Now, if the commissioning of the seventy-two were a movie, this is the part in the plot where you find a twist. As I read the passage of Scripture in Luke 10, I was awakened by the fact that the harvest is plentiful. I saw the need for more workers, and I understood the need to pray and ask the Lord to send out workers. Then the Lord commissioned the seventy-two with specific instructions. All seemed sequential and logical until I came to this section of the story. This is the part I did not expect in a commissioning of thirty-six teams of missionaries. The first half of this story seems to be about sharing the gospel, making disciples, and perhaps even starting churches if needed. But that is not all the disciples were to do. In fact, more is said about healing than making disciples. The disciples were sent to reverse the physical effects of evil with the power delegated to them.[67] They were to serve through healing diseases, weaknesses, or inabilities.[68] They were sent to make a tangible, real-time difference in the lives of those they served. They were there to deliver hope and healing.

Tiffany was determined. No one ever doubted that. Smart and hardworking, she could succeed at anything she put her mind to. Nothing was going to stop her. But life sure tried. Her father died when she was fifteen. Her mom died two years later. She was legally

[67] Swindoll, *Insights on Luke*, PDF ebook.
[68] Edwards, *The Gospel according to Luke*, 308.

declared an adult and was on her own. She struggled to get by but managed to enroll in Angelina College in Lufkin, Texas. Then she became involved in a bad relationship. Shortly after, her daughter, Kalista, was born. School would have to wait. Her daughter was what was most important. Tiffany started working full time, driving one hundred miles round-trip to make a living. As if Tiffany didn't have enough to balance, Kalista suffered through health issues. Numerous doctor visits forced Tiffany to miss work one too many times. She was fired—and desperate.

"I was a nervous wreck," she said. "I didn't know what to do. I had a daughter. I didn't have a job. I had no hope." She needed healing and hope. An uncle told her about Buckner Family Pathways. The solid foundation of Buckner provided the footing Tiffany needed to take the steps to begin her healing process and fulfill her potential. She quickly bonded with Buckner staff members who started out as professional caseworkers, turned into mentors, and are now what she desperately missed. "They've really become a family to us," she said. "My daughter's gotten to grow up [at Buckner Family Pathways]. We came just before her second birthday. This has become her family."

When Tiffany had a difficult time, Buckner staff members knew just what to say to keep her moving forward. Once when she and Kalista were sick, staff members brought them homemade soup. On other days, Tiffany received texts that staff members were praying for her. Kalista bonded with the other children on campus. She played with them daily, her giggles filling her home. "Seeing how these ladies work and seeing the difference they've made in my life, they've inspired me to want to work in social work. To be able to give back would be such a blessing."

Tiffany had some unexpected help one day when she was contemplating quitting school. She was walking through the social work building as she'd done hundreds of times when she noticed a plaque she hadn't before. "This name just jumped out at me," she said. "It was my mom's name. It was her signature from the honor society in 1993 when she had graduated. To me, it was God telling me, 'Your mom sees you and is proud of you. Keep going.'"

Tiffany finished an associate's degree and went on to receive her bachelor's degree in social work at Stephen F. Austin State University. Now she has her choice of jobs to support her daughter as she begins her postgraduate work. Her healing was a process.

Hope comes from the possibility of a better way, a healing. Hope shines when people are healed. The word for healing in New Testament Greek is *therapuo* meaning "therapy" or "process." The word used in Luke 10:9 by Jesus lends itself to a process of healing rather than an instantaneous or miraculous healing. Healing relationships, families, and communities brings hope. In Luke 10:8–9, it appears the command to heal precedes the command to preach.[69] The healings are a sign of the presence of the kingdom of God. Hope, peace, and healing is a process. In this case it starts with healing and serving. Preaching is to come later. Don't miss this. Serving comes before preaching. Healing comes before evangelism. Holistic ministry comes before church growth. The disciples were not confined to speaking to the sick; rather, they were to speak to everyone in the whole town.[70] The message was for all who would hear. The message of hope and healing was intended for every person in the community. But what about those seeking justice? Does the kingdom of Jesus have an answer for those who have been wronged?

---

[69] Marshall, *The Gospel of Luke*, 251.

[70] Blight, *An Exegetical Summary of Luke 1–11*, 455.

Questions to Consider

What kinds of healing do you think people need today?

How do peace and hope emerge from the possibility of healing?

What surprises you about Jesus' instructions to "heal the sick who are there"?

How does healing open opportunities for sharing the good news?

Have you ever experienced healing in your life or in the life of another person? If so, how did hope and peace emerge?

Chapter 6

HOPE AND JUSTICE

Seek first his kingdom and his righteousness, and all these things
will be given to you as well.

—Matthew 6:33

The subtitle of this book is *Peace, Healing, and Justice When the
Kingdom Comes Near.* Hope points to peace and healing found in the
kingdom. Peace and healing are evident in Luke 10:1–9, but justice
is not so evident in that passage. Justice is part of what the King
provides in His kingdom for all the King's subjects. He provides
justice and makes things just for each of us. The verse that comes
to mind is Matthew 6:33. Jesus tells us to seek, go after, and pursue
the kingdom of God and His righteousness, and the promise is that
everything else we hope for, long for, and need will be added to us.
It is a matter of priority setting. Seek the kingdom first. But the
word *justice* does not appear in this verse. So where does it come
from? How does one seek the justice of God while also seeking
the kingdom of the God? What is the relationship between the
kingdom and God's justice? Can you seek His kingdom and not His
justice? Must we seek both His kingdom and His justice to realize
that all these things will be added to us?

My Spanish Bible sheds light on the interpretation of this verse.
In Spanish, Matthew 6:33 says: "Busquen primeramente el reino de
Dios y su justicia." Literally, this verse in Spanish says, "Seek first
the kingdom of God and His justice." The New Testament Greek

word translated righteousness is *dikaiosuné*. However, the same word for righteousness in the Septuagint (the Greek translation of the Hebrew text) is most often translated as justice.[71] A more accurate translation of Matthew 6:33 would be, "Seek first the kingdom of God and His justice, and all these things will be added to you." Jesus, the Lord and King, loves justice. In fact, one might argue in this context that the atonement of Jesus can be thought of as the greatest intervention of God's justice in history. His intervention on our behalf was characterized by restorative and retributive justice. The agenda of the kingdom is to restore justice and peace.[72]

There are four words used in the Bible for the concept of justice (two in Hebrew and two in Greek), appearing 1,060 times. One of the Hebrew words is *tsedaqah*, meaning delivering community-restoring justice.[73] Communities I have visited in the US and around the world need the delivery of justice for the community to be restored: the kind of justice that makes things right for the citizens, the families, and the children of the community. Peace, healing, and justice are what we can expect when the kingdom comes near to these communities.

Matthew 6:33 has been one of my life verses I memorized as a child. However, I never saw this verse in the context of justice. The second part of the verse is a promise, a reassurance, that if we seek the kingdom of God and His justice as a priority, everything we need will be added to us. The kingdom of God and His justice must become my personal priority. While I have focused on making the

---

[71] G. Cray, "A Theology of the Kingdom," in *Mission as Transformation: A Theology of the Whole Gospel*, eds. Vinay Samuel and Chris Sugden (Oxford: Regnum Books International, 1999), 35.

[72] Ibid., 36

[73] Glen H. Stassen and David P. Gushee, *Kingdom Ethics: Following Jesus in Contemporary Context* (Downers Grove, IL: IVP Academic 2003), 345.

kingdom first, have I also focused on seeking God's justice too? Or has my heart been mute to this issue of God's justice in the world? Is His justice a priority for me? As I write these lines, I pause to reflect and wonder if I have been ignorant to this issue or paid less attention to it. What does this concept of seeking God's justice as a priority mean for my personal sense of ethics as a follower of Jesus? I hope you stop with me for a moment and reconsider this verse for your life, your ethics, and your priorities today.

In order for us to process this concept adequately for our lives, we must consider questions about the concept of justice as it relates to hope, peace, and healing. What did justice mean in the first century? Why does justice matter? How does this concept of justice seeking impact my ethics as a follower of Jesus? How do hope and justice connect in the context of the kingdom? How do hope, peace, and healing relate to justice?

Justice in the First Century

Justice was rare for mistreated individuals in the first century. In Graeco-Roman society, the infant mortality rate was high, women did not have many rights, unwanted babies were commonly thrown into the trash heap, slaves were considered as objects by the owner, wives were considered strangers in the family and on the periphery until and only when they bore a son, and the poor were commonly mistreated.[74] Jesus lived in our world and saw the level of injustice taking place in the communities in which He lived. He was familiar with the words of the prophet Micah: "He has shown you, O mortal, what is good. And what does the LORD require of you? To act justly and to love mercy and to walk humbly with your God" (Micah 6:8). Jesus understands the basic expectations God has for

---

[74] Bruce Malina, *The New Testament World: Insights from Cultural Anthroplogy*, Third Edition (Louisville: Westminster John Knox Press, 2001).

His people: to behave justly, to love the mercy of God, and to live a humble life. Jesus carried these ideals deeply in His heart, in His words, and through His actions. In fact, He confronted the teachers of the Law and the Pharisees by calling them hypocrites, saying to them, "You give a tenth of your spices—mint, dill, and cumin. But you have neglected the more important matters of the law—justice, mercy and faithfulness. You should have practiced the latter, without neglecting the former. You blind guides! You strain out a gnat but swallow a camel" (Matthew 23:23–24). Jesus was very concerned about justice. He was willing to confront the religious leaders of His day publicly.

The biblical text lists four dimensions of justice: deliverance of the poor and powerless from an injustice that they regularly experience; lifting the foot of the domineering power off the neck of the dominated and oppressed; stopping violence and establishing peace; and restoring outcasts, the excluded, the Gentiles, the exiles, and the refugees to community.[75] When Jesus spoke for the first time in a worship setting as recorded in Luke 4, He read from the prophet Isaiah. He outlined His agenda for His ministry: to preach good news to the poor, to proclaim freedom for the prisoners and recovery of sight to the blind, to release the oppressed, and to proclaim the year of the Lord's favor. Sixteen of the seventeen kingdom-deliverance passages in Isaiah announced that justice was a key characteristic of God's kingdom.[76] The theme of justice was prevalent in the teaching of the prophets in the Old Testament. Isaiah was Jesus' go-to prophet for themes in His teaching and preaching. He referred to Isaiah's writings often in His teachings. The concept of justice was central to Isaiah's message. Justice was a big deal to Jesus. Should it also matter to us today?

---

[75] Glen H. Stassen and David P. Gushee, *Kingdom Ethics: Following Jesus in Contemporary Context* (Downers Grove, IL: InterVarsity Press, 2003), 349.

[76] Ibid.

Why Does Justice Matter?

Justice matters to us first because it matters to God. In the Scriptures there are over one thousand teachings on the topic of justice that often are ignored by people in the Christian faith.[77] Justice in the kingdom of Jesus means the King will ensure you are respected and treated with dignity and fairness, and He will prevent or reverse any injustice. It means your voice matters and is heard. As a citizen of the kingdom, you have a voice that matters, a voice that represents the wishes of the King. Justice in the kingdom means you matter to the King. Your well-being, your welfare, your best interest, and your purpose in the kingdom are protected and guarded. Themes of justice connect to the experience of the poor, the hungry, and the powerless from injustice as dominated and oppressed people.[78] Jesus came announcing the kingdom of God in His preaching. I cannot imagine a kingdom of Jesus without justice for all its inhabitants. Wherever the kingdom is, justice should be there too. If the King lives in us, justice should matter to us because it matters to the King. We want justice for ourselves. Surely nobody wants to be treated unjustly or denied justice. The challenge for us comes in the application of justice to other people in addition to a sense of justice for our own lives.

Jesus told a story about a servant who owed a great debt to illustrate justice as a part of the culture of the kingdom. The servant owed ten thousand talents, an amount impossible to repay as a day laborer. So the master was willing to work things out with him and told the servant to sell himself, his wife, and his children into slavery as well as sell all he had. This action would satisfy the debt. After hearing this dreadful news, the servant fell to the ground on his knees and

---

[77] Stassen and Gushee, *Kingdom Ethics*, 345.
[78] Ibid., 349–356.

pleaded, "Be patient with me and I will pay back everything." This offer was absurd. The servant would have to work seventy-two hours a week for two hundred thousand years with day-laborer wages to make enough money to pay off the debt. The master had pity on the servant, canceled the debt, and let him go.

The servant left the master's dwelling and went out into the streets and ran into one of his fellow servants that owed him one hundred denarii, which would amount to about $11,000 today. While this amount is steep, it would be possible to repay this amount at a cost of one fourth of a servant's income in one year. As soon as the servant who had just been forgiven saw his fellow servant, he grabbed him by the neck and began to choke him and said, "Pay back what you owe me!" The fellow servant fell to his knees and begged him, "Be patient with me, and I will pay it back." But the servant who had been forgiven refused. Instead, he had his fellow servant thrown into prison until he could pay the debt. When the master heard what happened, he said to his servant, "You wicked servant. I canceled all the debt of yours because you begged me to. Shouldn't you have had mercy on your fellow servant just as I had on you?" In anger, the master turned the servant over to the jailer to be tortured until he could repay the debt. Essentially, this amounts to a life sentence of repetitive torture.

Jesus ends the story by saying, "This is how my heavenly Father will treat each of you unless you forgive your brother or sister from your heart" (Matthew 18:23–35). This story is about how the kingdom works regarding justice and forgiveness. It teaches us we must forgive those who harm us, or we will not be forgiven for the way we have mistreated others. Justice in the kingdom of Jesus not only relates to our relationship to the King, but it also impacts our relationships with others like our family members, our friends, neighbors, and coworkers.

Justice Seeking and Personal Ethics

If seeking the kingdom of God and the justice of God should be my highest priority, how should I live this question out? What does this look like in everyday life? How does it apply to me and to those in my circle of influence? Perhaps reframing Matthew 6:33 and leaving out the kingdom for just a moment may help bring this priority into focus. Jesus said, "Seek first . . . his righteousness [the justice of God], and all these things will be given to you as well." What does this mean? How do we do this?

Ethics for the Christian, the follower of Jesus, is unique and apart from secular ethics. The field of Christian ethics did not appear until three hundred years after the death of Jesus. Early Christian writers were interested in ethics to refute the claims against them since their spiritual practices were misinterpreted and misunderstood by the society of their day.[79] The context and background for ethical behavior in relation to others, especially mistreated individuals, can be found in the teachings of Moses in the Book of Deuteronomy. The word *Deuteronomy* means second law and is also called "the book of teaching." In fact, Deuteronomy is a book of speeches, sermons, and discourses of Moses in the last few weeks of his life and looks toward Israel's life in the Promised Land. While Deuteronomy is a book of laws, it plays a major role in the development of Jewish theology and goes beyond the subject to point to religious and ethical implications and appeals to faith and obedience. The whole Book of Deuteronomy deals primarily with matters of belief and attitude.

In Deuteronomy, Moses is speaking to the children of slaves. His audience represents the next generation poised to move into the land they learned about as children. Keep in mind, Moses led a

---

[79] Kyle D. Fedler, *Exploring Christian Ethics: Biblical Foundations for Morality* (Louisville: Westminster John Knox Press, 2006), 8.

whole generation of slaves out of Egypt, across the Red Sea, and into the desert, where he gave them the Law. Now he pauses prior to crossing the Jordan River as the next generation prepares to cross into prosperity and blessing. For his last words, Moses reiterates the teaching of the law through a series of sermons, speeches, and homilies. Now, if you were Moses and you came to the end of your life with one more opportunity to provide wisdom and teaching through your last words, what would you say? What laws would you highlight? What would be salient to a people about to enter a land flowing with milk and honey? Moses chose to address issues of slavery, prosperity, and justice for those who would inherit the Promised Land.

Slavery

Now, this picture may be hard to visualize in our mind's eye primarily because most of us have no idea what slavery means from a personal perspective. Most of us have not had to experience being owned by another human being. We have not experienced what it feels like to be treated as though we were less than human. We may not know what it is like to serve the needs of another human every waking moment of every day of our lives under harsh treatment, brutality, and abuse. Slavery in our nation's history has been a nightmare. Even today, more than fourteen thousand[80] slaves are imported into this country every year through human trafficking. Most of these children are sold in the East and West Coasts of the US. It may be a real struggle to understand slavery in the twenty-first century. Slavery may not be in your family history, but many of us may find a

---

[80] Christian Sabyan, Emily Smith, and Manav Tanneeru, "Trafficking and the US," CNN, June 17, 2011, http://thecnnfreedomproject.blogs.cnn.com/2011/06/17/trafficking-and-the-u-s/.

history of poverty if we go back far enough and look carefully at the world around us and the way human beings treat each other.

Prosperity

Prosperity is not so much a stranger. Most of us are familiar with prosperity or what we might call the Promised Land. The Promised Land was a place where the children of slaves were going to be free: free to pursue their dreams, their hopes, and their aspirations. The Promised Land was a place where there would be plenty to eat, a place full of opportunity to work, to start a family, to enjoy life. Our nation, with all its faults and shortcomings, is that kind of place. We live in the land where many people have an opportunity to pursue a dream, a vision, start a family, enjoy work, and experience prosperity. We live in the land of three or more meals a day. We live in contrast to those who live on less than a dollar a day for survival. Moses's words to those living in the land of plenty may be a good word to those of us who have lived a life of privilege. Moses could not have known there would be 150 million orphans in the world today,[81] but the Lord of redemption did. Moses could not have known that undocumented immigration and global migration would be an issue in our world, but the Lord of redemption knew. Yet the Lord of redemption is still at work today with a keen eye toward the experience of the immigrant, the orphan, and the widow. If these issues are of concern to the Lord, should they be issues of concern for those who live to serve and please Him? What do these concepts of justice have to do with us today? How should we relate to the less fortunate in our communities, in our global village?

---

[81] "UN Data on the Plight of Children Worldwide," Children's Statistics, SOS Children's Villages, accessed February 11, 2019, https://www.sos-usa.org/our -impact/focus-areas/advocacy-movement-building/childrens-statistics.

Deuteronomy 24 records Moses's instructions from his last words regarding the fatherless, the widow, and the alien. He issues a call to justice for future inhabitants of the Promised Land.

A Call to Justice

In Deuteronomy 24:17–22, one of Moses's key messages was a plea, a call, to those entering the Promised Land, to uphold justice and not allow justice to be perverted, especially for the fatherless, the widow, and the alien. Moses taught that a citizen of the Promised Land must have a social and humane attitude toward the economically weak. He was concerned for the poor, the disadvantaged, indentured servants, escaped slaves, resident aliens, orphans, widows, and convicted criminals. He was concerned the alien would not have rights in a court of law, that the fatherless would not have a father to defend them in court, and that the widow's reputation would be at stake if her outer cloak was not returned to her by sundown.

Moses points back to their slavery in Egypt. He alludes to the story of Joseph and the unjust treatment on the part of his own brothers and with Potiphar's wife. Do you remember the betrayal by Joseph's brothers that caused him to be sold into slavery? Do you remember how he was falsely accused by Potiphar's wife and unjustly thrown into prison a second time (Genesis 37—41)? Moses wants the children of slaves entering the Promised Land to remember where they came from and to be careful not to repeat what was done to them. In other words He wants the pain of their past to serve as the passion for their future. Moses essentially says, "Don't forget the injustice, the abuse, the mistreatment, and the pain of your past so that when you are well off, when you become an owner, when you come into the land of prosperity, you will passionately insist on justice for the alien, the fatherless, and the widow."

Many of us have suffered some type of pain, mistreatment, injustice, and maybe even an abuse of some sort. We have suffered both insult and injury. We have been slighted, ridiculed, and mocked. Moses words remind us today that a call to justice means taking the pain of our past to bless others in the future. The truth is that we find our own healing when we prevent the abuse and injustice intended for others. If you ask the Lord to show you where injustice occurs in your community, it will become very clear to you. Will you allow yourself to be moved to do something about it? Will you consider ways to bring hope to those who suffer injustice?

Hope and Justice in the Context of the Kingdom

The King is in the kingdom. Where the King is, the kingdom is also. If King Jesus lives in our hearts, the kingdom should be evident wherever we make our lives in community. The community of the redeemed should manifest the reality of the kingdom with every effort to please the King. This truth may be simple and evident to us now as we look back to the first century, but it was not so evident to the followers of Jesus. N. T. Wright says in his book *How God Became King*, "Part of the meaning of the kingdom, in the four Gospels, is precisely the fact that it bursts upon Jesus' first followers as something so shocking as to be incomprehensible."[82] I can understand why believers today may not commonly understand the kingdom twenty-one centuries after Jesus walked this earth and first spoke of His Father's kingdom. The first disciples were expecting Jesus to restore geopolitical dominance over the Graeco-Roman world. They could reconcile the concepts of the kingdom and the coming of the Cross of Christ. In fact they were to become "a community rescued by the

---

[82] N. T. Wright, *How God Became King: The Forgotten Story of the Gospels* (New York: HarperCollins Publishers, 2012), 197.

cross and transformed into kingdom-bringers"[83] to the communities in which they lived. As kingdom-bringers, we bring hope to those around us. We model our lives after the king and offer justice and hope to those in our community, in our circle of influence. Christ is our life model.[84] We are called, as disciples of Christ, to live a life of self-denial and cross-bearing.[85] In doing so, we bring the kingdom near. The cross-bearing way is the way of love and life.[86] It is the way of Jesus. When we are confronted with an injustice, we bring hope as we act to make a difference. It will cost us something. It will cost us self-denial and maybe even some suffering to stand with the poor, the weak, the defenseless, the vulnerable child, the orphan, and the struggling family.

We bring hope and speak of hope when we encounter people in need. We bring our vision of hope because of the "power of God to bring life and newness out of death and darkness."[87] We bring the kingdom near and reverse situations of injustice and wrong-doing, and we provide solutions for people to live better lives. When justice is done, people have hope there can be a better future. Proverbs 21:15 says, "When justice is done, it brings joy to the righteous but terror to evildoers." Hope comes when justice appears. Hope shines when things are made right in the community, in families, and in relationships. Hope and justice come when the kingdom comes near.

---

[83] Ibid., 203.

[84] James M. Gustafson, *Christ and the Moral Life* (Chicago: The University of Chicago Press, 1968), 159.

[85] Ibid., 165.

[86] Ibid., 186.

[87] Fedler, *Exploring Christian Ethics*, 137.

Hope and Justice for the Family

Hector's home in the middle of June was hot, dusty, and cramped. Tattered bed sheets tried to block the blazing South Texas sun coming through the small square windows. Dirty dishes piled high in the sink, spilling onto the counter and the stove. As a single parent with four children, it's hard to find time to keep up with the housework. Hector has been a single dad of Hector Jr., fourteen, Rene, eleven, Sandy, seven, and Tania, six, for the past five years. He used to live in a tiny, trailer-like home he slowly assembled by himself to give his four children a safe place to live. Raising four children alone is hard, but not being able to work because the youngest isn't school-aged made it even harder. A trained mechanic, he did odd jobs when he could but struggled to make ends meet. He was living in a makeshift home on a lot purchased with a down payment with incredibly high interest rates. Land owners in an undeveloped part of the city near McAllen, Texas, had the freedom to sell parcels of land through an owner-financed arrangement with very high interest. Hector lived with the reality that missed payments would result in an eviction from the land, leaving his family homeless.

Hector heard about Buckner International from his neighbors in Peñitas, Texas. It took him a long time to muster up the courage to ask for help, but when he did, he found it immediately. He caught up to Ricardo Brambila, who was serving at the time as director of the local Buckner Family Hope Center, one day in the parking lot and explained his situation. Ricardo talked to him about being a single dad, the classes offered at the Family Hope Center, and volunteer opportunities. Ricardo could see that Hector was determined to help his children. The following day, Hector went to the market event at the Family Hope Center. Later, he and his family also attended a Buckner Shoes for Orphan Souls back-to-school distribution, where the children each received a new pair of shoes. Shoes were the first step to life transformation.

Hector enrolled in family coaching and classes at the Family Hope Center to become a better father. He completed the Fatherhood 24/7 Initiative course, which teaches men about their identity, discipline, how to partner with their wives, and how to leave a legacy in their families. Since Hector completed classes and family coaching, he earned enough points to qualify for a new home built by teams working through Buckner International Domestic Missions. Hope finally showed up for Hector and his family.

Hope, Peace, and Healing Connected to Justice

Where there is justice, there is hope. Where there is justice, there is peace. Where there is justice, healing begins. I started this chapter pointing out the subtitle of this book: *Peace, Healing, and Justice When the Kingdom Comes Near.* Jesus instructed the teams of two to announce "peace to this house" when they met people in their homes. The peace they were announcing was the peace that comes from Jesus, the Prince of Peace. Jesus also gave instructions for the teams of two to "heal the sick who are there" when they were welcomed to a city. Jesus was also passionate about and interested in justice being restored for individuals, children, parents, and families. Jesus said, "Heal the sick who are there and tell them the kingdom of God is near." Our task today is no different. We are sent out into the harvest field of humanity, into tough situations where people need hope. We offer them peace, healing, and justice because the kingdom has come near. The kingdom has come near because we, as kingdom-bringers, have come near with the King residing within us. Peace, healing, and justice take place when the kingdom comes near. But how? How does this happen when the kingdom comes near? What does it mean today?

Questions to Consider

What is it about justice that makes hope a possibility?

What would it be like to seek first the justice of God?

Where do you find injustice in your community or circle of influence?

If the kingdom is near you, how should justice become a reality?

How does justice materialize when the kingdom comes near?

Chapter 7

HOPE WHEN THE KINGDOM COMES NEAR

Heal the sick who are there and tell them, "The kingdom of God has come near to you."

—Luke 10:9

Hope shines brightly when the kingdom comes near and when King Jesus is present. Jesus the King came preaching and teaching the kingdom of God, the kingdom of heaven, to those He spoke to and encountered. We see these concepts in His teaching and in the teaching of the apostles and in the early church. Jesus brought the kingdom during His ministry, and He also spoke of a kingdom in the future. His kingdom delivers a transformative impact and uniquely blends the heart of evangelism and social ministry for the here and now as well as the yet to be.

Hope shines when the kingdom comes near. The command of Jesus in Luke 10:9 is to "heal the sick who are there and tell them, 'The kingdom of God has come near to you.'" What does it mean for the kingdom to come literally near to those we serve? This question requires an exploration of who Jesus is as King and what His kingdom means in practical terms. It requires an inventory of what Jesus taught about the kingdom; a review of how the early church understood the kingdom; what an understanding of the kingdom means for evangelism and social ministry; how kingdom nearness brings life transformation; and how the kingdom can be realized now as well as in the future. So the journey begins with an exploration of the King and His kingdom.

The King and His Kingdom

Who is Jesus as King? What does His kingdom mean in practical terms? It may be useful here to outline the biblical foundations for Jesus as King and define what His kingdom means. Kingdom literally means "kingship," a relationship between the king and his subjects. What does it mean for followers of Jesus to follow Him as King and to live out the King's commands and instructions? To know Jesus as King may look different from knowing Him as Savior, Redeemer, and Lord. There are practical implications for living in relationship to a "king." What does it mean to live in a kingdom and serve a king or queen? Serving Jesus as King would resemble the weight, the responsibility, and the privilege of serving an earthly monarch with great consequence. Knowing what Jesus taught, lived, and demonstrated about the kingdom helps us know the King and His kingdom.

The origin for the idea of the kingdom of God can be traced to the covenant God made with the people of Israel who were to become a "kingdom of priests and a holy nation" as described in Exodus 19:5–6. This idea became a reality when King David became king of Israel.[88] The people of Israel had a king who ruled in splendor and majesty. When Jesus said, "kingdom of God," He was not referring to a geopolitical reality. Rather, he referred to a "fellowship of men with God and with one another in love."[89] Even so, it is challenging for us today to capture the essence of what it means to serve a king twenty-one centuries later.

You have heard the saying "for king and country." The idea is to serve the king or queen as a primary duty as well as serving the country. This idea became a war slogan during World War I when

---

[88] Alexander M. F. Macinnes, *The Kingdom of God in the Apostolic Writings* (London: James Clarke & Co. Ltd, 1924).

[89] Ibid., 42.

Britons were called up for duty. Within weeks of the war breaking out, Britain needed many more fighting men. A series of recruitment initiatives produced an unprecedented surge of volunteers. On September 3, 1914, Britain saw 33,204 young men answer the call to serve "king and country"—more on one day than the army normally recruited in a year.[90] Volunteers who served the military responded out of a sense of loyalty and patriotism to serve their king and country. To serve one meant to serve the other. Loyal subjects of the king were willing to lay down their lives in service to their king and country. So how does the idea of serving the king apply to Jesus?

Jesus, the King

Jesus never claimed the title of king during his ministry. Yet, others claimed this title for Him. Nathaniel, a follower of Jesus, once declared, "Rabbi, you are the Son of God; you are the king of Israel" (John 1:49). When the crowds met Jesus during His triumphal entry into Jerusalem, "they took palm branches and went out to meet Him, shouting 'Hosanna!' 'Blessed is He who comes in the name of the Lord!' 'Blessed is the king of Israel!'" (John 12:13). Pilate asked Jesus, "'Are you the king of the Jews?' 'You have said so,' Jesus replied" (Matthew 27:11). Pilate also had a sign placed on Jesus' Cross that said, "Jesus of Nazareth, the king of the Jews" (John 19:19). When John the apostle wrote his vision of Jesus as King from the island of Patmos, he wrote, "On his robe and on his thigh he has this name written: KING OF KINGS AND LORD OF LORDS" (Revelation 19:16). Even though Jesus did not claim this title, one can safely assume He was

---

[90] Andy McSmith, "A History of the First World War in 100 Moments: The call of King and country sees a rush to enlist," *The Independent*, April 10, 2014, http://www.independent.co.uk/news/world/world-history/history-of-the-first -world-war-in-100-moments/a-history-of-the-first-war-in-100-moments-the -call-of-king-and-country-sees-a-rush-to-enlist-9252418.html.

and is Jesus the King. If He is your King, the one who died for your salvation and your life, would you not be willing to give up your life for Him? Jesus taught, "For whoever wants to save their life will lose it, but whoever loses their life for me will find it" (Matthew 16:25). It is counterintuitive from a human perspective to find life by first losing it as a follower of Jesus. Yet this is the way of Jesus the King. Giving up one's life in service of the King leads to a discovery of the true meaning of life itself. You find life when you lose it for your King.

While Jesus did not claim the title of King, he taught about the kingdom of God and often referred to the kingdom of God as "my kingdom" (John 18:36). If we are to know Jesus as the king, what would that mean for us as his subjects? How would we regard Him? How would we serve Him? How would we seek to obey him? We know Jesus is King, but what do we know about His kingdom?

The Kingdom of Jesus

Jesus taught and preached much about the kingdom of God (Matthew 4:17). He also demonstrated the reality of the kingdom by overcoming nature, exorcising demons, healing people from disease, and raising people from the dead.[91] However, the idea of the kingdom of God was not a common expression in everyday language in the time of Jesus. It was only one of the many ways the Jews spoke about their hope for a new age—the eschatological age—when the new reign of God would come. In fact Jesus would not have told so many stories about the kingdom of God if it were commonly understood and if people knew exactly what He meant when He said "the kingdom of God is like."[92] When Jesus spoke

---

[91] Darrell Bock, *The NIV Application Commentary: Luke* (Grand Rapids: Zondervan, 1998).

[92] Cray, "A Theology of the Kingdom."

of the kingdom of God, He was not referring to a place. Rather, he was referring to a relationship. E. David Cook offers the idea of "kingship" to accentuate a living relationship with the King.[93] He adds that living in a relationship with a king affects the way we live. It means we live according to what the king wants, according to his will and under his authority and control. The key to this kind of relationship is membership in the kingdom and the quality of relationship with the King. We enter the kingdom by becoming obedient servants.[94] How does one know, see, or sense the kingdom has arrived if it is a kingship, a relationship? The kingdom of God is not a timeless reality or place; rather, it comes to us through the presence of Jesus and His disciples as is the case in Luke 10.[95] The kingdom is "the event of God's triumph, God's reign," and "happens where God's will is fulfilled. God rules where and when people forgive unconditionally and without limit, where and when the boundaries of justice are broken and the disenfranchised, the excluded, the neglected, or the forgotten are heard, included, cared for and remembered."[96] This kind of reign or rule of God happens when He first reigns in our heart through a relationship with Him. We know the kingdom has arrived when we enter a relationship with Jesus the King. In summary Jesus brings the kingdom[97] when He comes to us and we receive Him.

This relationship with Jesus the King impacts us and all other relationships. In fact the whole message of the Bible is focused on God's relationship with humans and their relationship with

---

[93] Cook, *Living in the Kingdom.*

[94] Ibid.

[95] Marshall, *The Gospel of Luke*, 476.

[96] Mary Ann Getty-Sullivan, *Parables of the Kingdom: Jesus and the Use of Parables in the Synoptic Tradition* (Collegeville, MN: Liturgical Press), PDF ebook.

[97] Cook, *Living in the Kingdom*, 13.

each other. Kingdom nearness redefines our relationship with God through Jesus Christ, and it also redefines relationship with other people. The kingdom, as kingship, and as relationship, also redefines social relationships both formal and informal. The kingdom causes us to rethink our relationship with civil authority, national identity, relationships with the poor, with money, and with marriage relationships.[98] These relationships come under the rule of God in our lives. Jesus sums up the basic rule for living, often referred to as the Golden Rule (Matthew 7:12). This rule existed before Jesus taught it. However, it existed in the negative form: "Do not do unto others what you do not want them to do to you." Jesus took this negative principle and turned it into a positive. He indicated a proactive approach. He encouraged His followers to take the initiative to do good. Cook has rightly noted, "There is a big difference between refraining from doing harm to effectively looking for ways to do good."[99] A closer examination of the kingdom of God according to how Jesus spoke, taught, and demonstrated brings a sharper focus to what Jesus understood, meant, and communicated about His kingdom.

The Kingdom According to Jesus

What did Jesus say and teach about the kingdom? The very first words of Jesus in the Gospel of Mark, the earliest of the Gospels to be written, proclaim the arrival of the "kingdom of God."[100] On many occasions Jesus said, "The kingdom of God is like," and told a parable, a short story, to describe the kingdom. A parable is literally "a throwing or placing of things side by side, with the suggestion of comparison. . . . an earthly story with a heavenly

---

[98] Ibid., 39–53.

[99] Cook, *Living in the Kingdom*, 43.

[100] Ibid., 5.

meaning . . . a picture of things seen, intended to reveal and explain things unseen."[101] He shows the many facets and dimensions of the kingdom. The notion that there is one way, one model, to think and know about the kingdom will not suffice. It is critical to review the teachings of Jesus regarding the kingdom to understand what Jesus taught about His kingdom, its principles, and its way of living. How can we talk about, know, and understand what the kingdom is if we do not know what Jesus taught and did about it? How did the earliest followers of Jesus think, act, and believe about the kingdom of Jesus?

Jesus came preaching the kingdom of heaven at the outset of His ministry. He began His ministry preaching, "Repent, for the kingdom of heaven has come near" (Matthew 4:17). The phrase of the people in the time of Jesus was the "kingdom of God," cast in a political sense. However, Jesus took the phrase of the people "the kingdom of God" (also referred to as the "kingdom of heaven") and made it the central theme of His teaching, free from all political limitations.[102] This teaching must have had an impact on His followers.

The Kingdom in the Early Church

I wonder how Jesus' teaching about the kingdom impacted His immediate followers and those that followed in the early church. What did the early church, starting with the disciples and followers of Jesus, say about the kingdom? How did the early church fathers reflect on the idea of the kingdom? How did the early church practice and live out the kingdom way of life in practical and ethical terms? Knowing how the disciples, early followers, and early church fathers spoke, taught, and lived out Jesus' teaching on the kingdom provides guidance for how we can live out the kingdom today. What

---

[101] G. Campbell Morgan, *The Parables of the Kingdom* (New York: Fleming H. Revell Company, 1907), 13–14.

[102] Macinnes, *The Kingdom of God in the Apostolic Writings*, 15.

are the implications of what the early church believed regarding the spreading of the gospel and serving the poor?

The phrase, "the kingdom of God," appears in the Gospels of Matthew, Mark, Luke, and John 111 times, eight times in the Acts of the Apostles, fourteen times in the letters of the Apostle Paul, four times in the other epistles, and twice in the Book of Revelation. The overwhelming mention of the "kingdom of God" is found in the Gospel accounts.[103] In the Gospel according to Matthew, the concept of the kingdom is prominent. Matthew 6:33 records Jesus' teaching to "seek first his kingdom and His righteousness [justice], and all these things will be given to you as well." Matthew signaled the top priority of the kingdom and made this theme clear in the Beatitudes of Jesus recorded in Matthew 5:3–10. In Matthew 13 the Gospel writer recorded a series of seven parables on the kingdom followed by a second set of parables in Matthew 21:28—22:14, but the most powerful teaching on the kingdom is found in Matthew 25:31–46 with the parable of the sheep and goats.[104]

The decrease of the use of this phrase outside of the Gospels may be attributed to the context in which the early church existed. During this time there were frequent revolts against the Roman Empire. Thus apostolic leaders and followers of Christ chose to use this phrase less frequently to avoid suspicion and provocation by Roman officials.[105] Nevertheless, the disciples of Jesus and the writers of the New Testament used "the kingdom of God" as a concept in their teaching and writing, thus forming a framework for faith and practice in the early church.

---

[103] Ibid., 16.

[104] Benedict T. Viviano, *The Kingdom of God in History* (Wilmington, DE: Michael Glazier Inc., 1988).

[105] Macinnes, *The Kingdom of God in the Apostolic Writings,* 17.

Benedict Viviano, in studying how the early church fathers wrote about the kingdom of God, suggests that the concept of the "kingdom of God" falls into four broad categories: the eschatological stream, the spiritual-mystical stream, the political stream, and the ecclesial stream.[106]

The eschatological stream sees the kingdom as a future hope. Clement wrote about the kingdom in AD 95 and mentioned the hope of the kingdom in a Christian homily called Second Clement in AD 150.[107] The earliest Christian manual of teaching, called the Didache or Teaching of the Twelve Apostles and dated AD 50–70, mentions the kingdom in the Lord's prayer for the first time.[108] The greatest writer among the apostolic fathers was Ignatius of Antioch, a bishop and martyr who wrote about the kingdom of God between AD 108 and 117.[109] Polycarp, an early church father, wrote a letter to the Philippians in which he mentioned the kingdom of God before his death in AD 155.[110] It is clear that the early church fathers who saw the kingdom as future hope thought, spoke, and wrote about the concept of the kingdom of God.

The spiritual mystical stream of apostolic writers saw the kingdom as a spiritual good in the soul of the believer. The greatest example came from Origen of Alexandria, between AD 185–254. His goal was to follow the Apostles Paul and John to take Christianity beyond the mental horizons of Judaism.

The political stream saw the kingdom of God on earth with a political structure. Constantine the Great, who died in AD 337 and claimed to have converted to the Christian faith, attempted to turn the

---

[106] Viviano, *The Kingdom of God in History,* 30–48.

[107] Ibid., 32–33.

[108] Ibid., 33.

[109] Ibid., 33–34.

[110] Ibid., 34.

whole Roman empire into a Christian empire. Eusebius of Caesarea, an early church father who lived between AD 200–340, served as the spiritual advisor to Constantine and wrote about the monarch of God.[111]

The ecclesial stream saw the kingdom of God on earth within the church. Augustine, Bishop of Hippo who lived between AD 354–430, wrote about the city of God, the longest single book ever written about the kingdom of God.[112]

The theme of the kingdom of God, even though used and interpreted in various ways, was a common theme among the early church fathers through the first five hundred years of the existence of the church. Given the teaching of Jesus, the writings of New Testament authors, and the early church fathers, how does evangelism and social ministry blend?

The Kingdom as Life Transformation

Can these two areas of focus, evangelism and social ministry, represent two sides of the same coin as evidenced in Luke 10:1–9? Those who champion evangelism over social ministry may cite the priority of the soul in the next life as the top priority for ministry. Those who champion social ministry may prioritize the daily needs of the person in the here and now with utmost importance. Jesus valued both, teaching and modeling this approach. He raises the bar of what a transformed life from among the disadvantaged would look like. In fact Samuel and Sugden affirm that both evangelism and social responsibility have always been practiced since the New Testament church. They argue that no mission agency before the twentieth century ever stated as its only legitimate mission activity

---

[111] Ibid., 47.

[112] Ibid., 48.

the verbal proclamation of the gospel.[113] It was in practical terms the Christian mission that introduced literacy, education, medicine, and technology, and opposed child marriage and drunkenness. Mission work has always included activities to bring about personal and social change. Samuel and Sugden argue that the very basis for personal change is the establishment of a new society, which is an element of social change.[114] We expect to see life transformation through our work at Buckner because we are bringing the King's kingdom near.

What happens to a life broken by sin when the kingdom comes near? What does life transformation look like when the King and His kingdom connect with a wounded person in need of peace, healing, and justice? A metamorphosis takes place. Everything changes. Their story of what the king has done and is doing in their life reads like current events rather than a conversion story many years prior. What does the peace of Christ look like in this person's life *now*? What kind of impact does relational healing have on a person, a family, a community *now*? What does life transformation look like when justice appears in a person's life experience *now*? Is it possible to experience the transformed life *now*, or do we have to wait until we reach the afterlife?

The Kingdom Now and Yet to Be

Is the kingdom meant for today, or is it something we look forward to? Jesus said, "Heal the sick who are there and tell them, 'The kingdom of God has come near to you.'" His command points to a present-tense reality. Kingdom reality is not so much the idea of a kingdom as in a place but the presence of the King. He is with us now, but there is

---

[113] V. Samuel and C. Sugden, "Evangelism and Social Responsibility: A Biblical Study on Priorities," in *In Word and Deed: Evangelism and Social Responsibility*, ed. Bruce Nichols (London: Paternoster Press), 191.

[114] Ibid., 211.

more of Jesus to come when we are with Him forever. How are things different when Jesus is with us? He has come near to us and wants to come near to others, yet His coming is not all that it will be when we are with Him forever. Since we are not in a perfect state of the kingdom in this life, we have more kingdom living to look forward to. To some degree the kingdom is here *now*, and we also look forward to a final time when we will be in a "state of the kingdom" reality in the presence of the King every day and in every situation.

The phrase, "the kingdom of God," refers to an eschatological concept, the study of future things, that first appears in the prophets in the Old Testament and later at the time of the exile. Eschatology refers to a future world thought of as a time and place when all human hopes will be fulfilled according to God's purposes. Micah, the prophet, thought of the kingdom of God (God's rule) as a time when there would be peace among all nations.[115] The kingdom sounds very exciting and carries with it much promise. Yet is it for today, or must we wait until a future time when all things will be made new? To answer this question, a summary of three major theological views on this subject may help. The works of Oscar Cullmann, Jürgen Moltmann, and Wolfhart Pannenberg[116] help us gain a point of reference as to the present or future sense of the kingdom of God.

---

[115] Getty-Sullivan, *Parables of the Kingdom,* PDF ebook.

[116] Oscar Cullmann was a Christian theologian in the Lutheran tradition best known for his work in the ecumenical movement and his part in establishing a dialogue between Lutheran and Roman Catholic traditions. Jürgen Moltmann is a German Reformed theologian serving as professor emeritus of Systematic Theology at the University of Tübingen, Germany. Wolfhart Pannenberg was a German theologian who made significant contributions to modern theology, including the concept of history as a form of revelation centered on the resurrection of Jesus Christ. See https://en.wikipedia.org/wiki/Oscar_Cullmann; https://en.wikipedia.org/wiki/Jürgen_Moltmann; https://en.wikipedia.org/wiki/Wolfhart_Pannenberg.

Oscar Cullman sees redemptive history, the story of salvation, as linear, heading toward the end times, the things to come. He sees redemptive history in the Old Testament as pointed to Jesus Christ, the risen and crucified one, as the mid-point of redemptive history.[117] He sees the kingdom of God to be present and future. He sees the kingdom as the immediate nearness of the coming kingdom based in the present, already realized in Jesus. He contends that what is yet to come in the kingdom will come because the crucifixion of Jesus has already occurred. He refers to his view as the salvation-historical tension.[118] He points to the power and evidence of the kingdom of God in the life and work of Jesus of Nazareth and yet focuses on the already-but-not-yet teachings of Jesus as well.

Jürgen Moltmann, on the other hand, views the kingdom as *tectum sub cruce*, hidden under the Cross. He looks to the kingdom of God as resurrection and new creation to be anticipated in the future. He emphasizes the anxious expectation of the whole creation that awaits the liberty of the children of God. For Moltmann, the kingdom of God is present as a promise and hope for the future horizon of all things. He sees the kingdom as a future culmination of history, but not now.[119]

Wolfhart Pannenberg does not see the kingdom of God as fulfilled and confronts the validity of God's lordship. He suggests the current condition of the world and the impact of sin rules out the presence of the kingdom of God. He argues that if the kingdom of God is not fulfilled in the current time, maybe God is not yet all powerful over all things. He suggests the lordship of God is a hope-for-future.

---

[117] Oscar Cullmann, *Christ and Time: The Primitive Christian Conception of Time and History*, rev. ed. (Eugene, OR: Wipf and Stock, 1962).

[118] Oscar Cullmann, *Salvation in History* (New York: Harper & Row, 1967).

[119] Jürgen Moltmann, *Theology of Hope: On the Ground and the Implications of a Christian Eschatology* (New York: Harper & Row, 1967), 222–224.

He expects a new heaven and a new earth as the coming kingdom to be established at some point in the future. Pannenberg views an end-time kingdom that ushers in a reconciliation of the individual and society and the fulfillment of human destiny. He argues that "this-worldly" utopia of social fulfillment achieved by human action is an imperfect expression of the hope of a future consummation of humanity.[120]

These three schools of thought interpret the kingdom of God in terms of time in different ways. Cullmann argues for an already-and-yet-to-be reality of the kingdom. Moltmann contends for a future kingdom not present now. Pannenberg argues that any attempt at the kingdom now is imperfect and a partial glimpse of a future kingdom that cannot exist now, but is only to be revealed in the new heaven and new earth at the end of human history. I believe the kingdom came in the life and work of Jesus of Nazareth, the Son of God. He brought the kingdom near in the incarnation, in His ministry, and through His disciples. He continues to move the kingdom to places where hope is needed and in lives that need healing, restoration, and redemption. Yet there is a greater sense of what the kingdom will be like when Jesus returns to reign forever. I believe the kingdom is possible now and there is much more kingdom living ahead of us.

I started this chapter making the case for the kingdom of God in the *here and now* as well as the *yet to be*. I agree with Cullmann that Jesus is the mid-point of redemptive history marked by His birth, life, ministry, death, and Resurrection. Jesus brought the kingdom near when He healed people, when He raised people from the dead, when He cast out demons from demon-possessed individuals, when He forgave a woman caught in adultery and challenged her to go and sin no more in a new life (John 8:1–11), when He met a Samaritan

---

[120] Wolfhart Pannenberg, *Systematic Theology*, Vol. 3. (Grand Rapids: William B. Eerdmans Publishing Company, 2009), 580–586.

at the well and offered her living water (John 4:4–26), and when He redeemed the life of Zacchaeus and said, "Salvation has come to this house" (Luke 19:1–10). Jesus came preaching the kingdom and healing the sick. He also sent out His followers and disciples to bring peace, healing, and justice; to heal those they encountered; and to tell them the kingdom had come near. Jesus brought the kingdom and continues to do so. We have the hope that the kingdom life we live now will become even better when He returns.

The disciples, Gospel writers, the Apostle Paul, Luke in the Book of Acts, and John in his Revelation all referenced the kingdom of God. The early church fathers also referenced the kingdom of God in their writings. Even though contemporary theologians differ in their views of the kingdom in terms of time and the end times, they agree the kingdom is a realty, whether present or future. The kingdom of God is not bound by our concept of time or understanding of end times. My view is that the kingdom of God is both already now and yet to be in all its potential and majesty. Since the reality and tradition of the kingdom of God is so rich and pervasive, how would we experience the kingdom now, and how might we offer hope to people in our circle of influence? The next chapter answers those questions.

Questions to Consider

What does the kingdom mean to you?

How did Jesus talk about the kingdom during his three-year ministry?

What stands out about how the disciples of Jesus and early church fathers spoke and wrote about the kingdom?

Is the kingdom possible now? If so, how?

How can you and your friends participate in the kingdom now?

Chapter 8

HOPE AND THE KINGDOM NEAR YOU

Hope deferred makes the heart sick, but a longing fulfilled is a tree of life.

—Proverbs 13:12

You might need hope as you read this book. You might be facing an incredibly difficult situation you never dreamed of or thought possible. If the kingdom is near you, hope is not far. People around you may need hope too. They need hope now. To delay the possibility of hope is to make the heart sick. A heart that is sick needs healing. False hope raises expectations, disappoints, and leads to a worse situation than before. On the other hand, to provide hope when it is needed brings life to those in need.

The phrase "tree of life" in the Hebrew language is "tree of lives," conveying the idea that it comforts and invigorates both body and soul. It provides the healing for a sick heart. John, the apostle, wrote of the tree of life in his vision of heaven, saying, "Then the angel showed me the river of the water of life, as clear as crystal, flowing from the throne of God and of the Lamb down in the middle of the great street of the city. On each side of the river stood the tree of life, bearing twelve crops of fruit, yielding its fruit every month. And the leaves of the tree are for the healing of the nations" (Revelation 22:1–2). In the kingdom, the King brings healing and hope for its inhabitants and for the nations. I came to the realization that healing and hope must not be deferred in the work that I do leading

Buckner International. We provide services to all vulnerable people: children, orphans, families, and senior adults. Over the past twelve years, I have yet to engage a vulnerable child, an orphan child, a struggling family, or senior adult who did not need hope right at that moment.

Hope is "ultimate Christian hope" that points the way toward the possibility of change, rescue, transformation, and new possibilities within the world in the present.[121] Hope is possible because the kingdom is near. But does this truth of kingdom nearness reverberate in our minds, our relationships, and our daily experience? Have you thought about the kingdom near you? Have you thought of the kingdom coming near through your church? Have you considered the kingdom coming near in the wider community of Jesus?

The Kingdom Near You

The kingdom of God is near you because the King is in you. The King of Glory, the Prince of Peace, Jesus Himself, through His Spirit lives in you if you have placed your trust and faith in Him as your Lord and Savior. Where the King lives is where His kingdom exists. He is your King, your Lord, and your leader. The Apostle Paul wrote, "For, 'Who has known the mind of the Lord so as to instruct him?' But we have the mind of Christ" (1 Corinthians 2:16). We have the potential to think like the King as a part of His kingdom. After all, we can commune with God, understand His will, and grasp the foundational truths expressed in Scripture.[122] The kingdom is near because we have the potential to think like citizens of the kingdom. We want to do as the King does. We want

---

[121] N. T. Wright, *Surprised By Hope: Rethinking Heaven, the Resurrection, and the Mission of the Church* (New York: HarperOne, 2008), 5.

[122] Craig L. Bloomberg, *The NIV Application Commentary: First Corinthians* (Grand Rapids: Zondervan, 1994), 70.

to think like He thinks. We can think like He thinks because we have His mind in us. But do we? Do the objects of hope, peace, healing, and justice for others predominate our thinking, or do other, more earthly pursuits predominate our thinking? We live in two worlds simultaneously, but which one prevails in our thoughts? We are all dual citizens of the kingdom and of the country in which we live. But which one prevails or predominates? What happens when they collide? Which one rules? When conflict arises, where is our ultimate loyalty? The best scorecard of our priorities appears in our spending of time, money, and energy. What would your scorecard say about your loyalty to your King and His kingdom?

First Century Kingdom Nearness

Hope comes when the kingdom comes near. It happens when the kingdom is near you. It happened in the first century, and it happens today. Paul and Silas were on their way to the place of prayer in the city of Philippi when they were met by a slave girl who was possessed by a spirit enabling her to predict the future. She earned lots of money for her owners by fortune telling. When the slave girl saw Paul and Silas, she began shouting, "These men are servants of the Most High God, who are telling you the way to be saved" (Acts 16:17). She kept harassing them for several days. One day Paul turned to her and said to the demonic spirit in her, "In the name of Jesus Christ I command you to come out of her!" (v. 18). At that moment the spirit left her. But the owners were not happy because they realized their hope of making money from her was gone. They seized Paul and Silas and took them to the marketplace to face the authorities. Facing the magistrates, the owners accused Paul and Silas, saying, "These men are Jews, and are throwing our city into an uproar by advocating customs unlawful for us Romans to accept or practice" (vv. 20–21). The crowd joined in mob fashion against

Paul and Silas, and the magistrates ordered them to be stripped and beaten. After they were severely flogged, they were thrown into prison, and the jailer was commanded to guard them carefully. The jailer took Paul and Silas and placed them in the inner cell, deep into the prison, and fastened their feet in stocks so they could not move.

Paul and Silas were falsely accused, beaten, thrown in prison without a trial, and placed under high security surveillance after they brought healing to the slave girl possessed by a spirit. Sometimes when you bring healing and hope to people, it irritates other people who benefit from these unhealthy situations. The jailer of the prison guarded Paul and Silas. Someone once said, "Roman soldiers never die, they merely retire at Philippi."[123] The jailer survived a life of battle, war, and brutal dismemberment of his adversaries. If one survived such a career, he was awarded with an assignment as a jailer with a home built above the prison. This is where the jailer in Acts 16 and his family lived. In other words the jailer was a tough, seasoned war veteran with the scars to prove it. He was not someone you would want to meet in a dark alley late at night.

Paul and Silas, after being treated unjustly, spent their time in prayer and singing hymns to God with a captive audience of other prisoners who heard everything. About midnight a major earthquake shook the city, the prison, and the very cell where Paul and Silas were held, and the prison doors flew open. Everybody's chains came loose. The jailer knew he was personally responsible for all the prisoners in his custody and knew he would face execution if any of them escaped. The jailer woke up thinking the prisoners all escaped and drew his sword to take his own life when Paul called out to him and said, "Don't harm yourself! We are all here!" (v. 28). Acts then

---

[123] I first heard this phrase in the early 1990s from Thom Wolf, International President of the Thom Wolf Institute for Global Studies, in Los Angeles, California, during a training conference.

records, "The jailer called for lights, rushed in and fell trembling before Paul and Silas. He then brought them out and asked, 'Sirs, what must I do to be saved?' They replied, 'Believe in the Lord Jesus, and you will be saved—you and your household'" (vv. 29–31).

The next scene of this dramatic event was held in the jailer's house. The jailer must have taken Paul and Silas out of the prison and into his home where they spoke the Word of the Lord to the jailer and to all the others in his house. The jailer who was guarding these prisoners under high security has now taken them into his own home? Don't miss this point. Don't miss the transformation—the healing that is happening here on this rough and tough war veteran. At that very hour, the jailer took Paul and Silas and washed their wounds. This would have happened in the water fountain in the courtyard of his home. Why did the jailer not wash their wounds when they were first put in prison? I don't think it mattered to him. It was not until his heart opened to the Lord Jesus that he experienced a deep healing and began to think differently. Paul and Silas were no longer seen as lawbreakers but as brothers in the Lord. What could the jailer's family be thinking through this experience? They knew their father was a hardened soldier, a war veteran, a tough man capable of inflicting wounds, but now they observed him washing wounds of prisoners. What happened next is the kingdom coming near, the King showing up in the life of this first century family.

After the earthquake the jailer's family was awakened, perhaps fearful of the fate facing their father. But instead, the family saw their father bringing prisoners into the family courtyard where he began washing their wounds, maybe even asking family members for towels and bandages. They heard the good news of hope and healing, of forgiveness and restoration, of salvation and grace. They were so convinced of the transforming power of the good news of Jesus, as seen in their father's example, they received the faith and agreed to be baptized with their father at that moment. Hope had arrived. The kingdom came near to this family. The family had a new father. It was time to celebrate.

After the jailer and his family were baptized, they went into the jailer's home, and he served Paul and Silas a meal. I would not expect a man, a jailer, a war veteran, to serve food to anyone, not even his own family in the first century. He might order his wife to serve them, but instead he was serving a meal to prisoners. How radical is that? The king showed up and so did His kingdom. Hope, healing, peace, and justice all came crashing in to set this family straight, to make things right. This is what all families want: a serving father, a man with gentle strength, a man who has been forgiven and knows how to demonstrate grace toward his wife, his children, and his grandchildren. Has this happened in your family? Does the man of the house serve everyone who lives there? Does he show grace? Does he show a repentant heart? Does he serve his wife and children? Is he teachable? Does he admit when he is wrong? Does he know how to ask for forgiveness? Does he serve the stranger, the visitor, the guest? Does he demonstrate love publicly? Does the King rule in the heart of the man in your home? Has the kingdom shown up in your home? Has the King shown up in your home?

Twenty-First Century Kingdom Nearness

The kingdom showed up in full bloom in Jocotenango, Guatemala, a few years ago. I was leading a vision trip for prospective donors and friends of Buckner. Debbie Potter and Dana Stubblefield[124] traveled with me to Guatemala for a visit to see Buckner ministry

---

[124] Debbie Potter is the children's pastor at Trinity Baptist Church in San Antonio, Texas, and serves on the board of trustees at Buckner International. Dana Stubblefield serves the children's ministry at Trinity Baptist Church with Debbie and is a friend and supporter of the ministry of Buckner International.

in action. The staff arranged for us to see the work in Guatemala including our Family Hope Center in Jocotenango, a small village just outside of Antiqua. I traveled with Roberto Tejada, executive director of Buckner Guatemala, Buckner staff members from our Dallas Support Center, and other staff to this city with Debbie and Dana. We had a nice drive to Antiqua and then up to Jocotenango. We made an appointment to visit Dulce, a little girl who received the three-millionth pair of shoes the year prior from Buckner Shoes for Orphan Souls, commemorating a milestone over the past fifteen years for vulnerable and hurting children around the world. We were on our way to greet Dulce, to check on her, and to meet her family. We planned to take photos and maybe some video of this momentous occasion.

As we arrived at her home set up on a hill, my staff advised me that her father was there but was intoxicated. It was a defining moment for me. I did not want to endanger my guests, and I could not predict if he would be disruptive during the visit. I was unsure as to whether we should proceed. As we discussed the pros and cons of getting out of the van, my staff sent word from Maria Elena, Dulce's mother, saying, "Please get down and visit because we feel safe when you are here, and maybe you can pray for my husband." That word settled the matter for all of us. I whispered a prayer at that moment, asking the Lord to guide us, to be present, and to do something special for this precious family.

We unloaded the van and began to climb up the path to Dulce's home. Dulce and her sisters greeted us, took us by the hand, and joyfully led us up the trail to their home. Dulce's sister stopped us along the way to glance back at the city visible from the steps leading up to their home. They were so proud and so happy to show us where they lived. Once we entered the gate that led into the patio of their home, we saw a very large pig in a stall, broken toys littering the yard, and the home made of slats of old wood with holes in them covered by a tin roof that leaked when it rained. Maria Elena raised pigs for a living since her husband's job did not provide enough money to sustain the family. She would raise the pig, sell it for slaughter, and with the proceeds buy more piglets, pay her bills, and buy food for the family. Maria Elena invited us into her home where she showed us the limited furniture she had. She was so proud of a new dresser they had received where clean clothes were neatly folded. Prior to that time, she used to store the neatly folded clothes on the dirt floor. The girls showed us some of the new furniture Buckner had given them and the place where they studied. Dulce's father was on hand but did not disturb our visit. He was present yet fully intoxicated. Our staff interacted with him to ensure he was not disruptive. He seemed harmless in my estimation.

We spent some time playing with the girls, taking pictures, and interacting with Maria Elena to learn about their situation. At one point, I thought it was time to wrap up our visit, so I told Maria Elena it was about time to go.

"Don't forget, you are going to pray before you leave," she responded.

I gathered Debbie and Dana, our staff, and the family in a circle to pray.

"Is there something you would like for us to pray about before we leave?" I asked Maria Elena.

"Yes, I have three things I would like to ask prayer for," she responded.

I was not prepared to hear her petition.

"First, I would like to ask you to pray for me as I am learning how to read in Spanish. My life's dream is to be able to read the Bible for myself."

Honestly, her prayer request took me by complete surprise. I was expecting her to ask for financial support, food, or maybe even new furniture. Her priority and first request was to learn how to read, to not give up learning Spanish, so she could one day read the Bible herself. I was stunned, shocked, and convicted. I have Bibles in several languages, including English, Greek, Hebrew, Spanish, and Portuguese, but could not recall my hunger for the Scriptures on par with Maria Elena's desire to read them. I was choked up, perhaps with guilt. I could not speak. I did all I could to translate to Debbie and Dana.

After I tried desperately to regain my composure, I spoke again to Maria Elena.

"OK, we will pray for you to learn how to read in Spanish. What is your second request for prayer?" I asked.

"Please pray that our housing situation would improve," she said. "We are in an unstable situation."

Without knowing more facts, I agreed to pray for their home environment as well. I felt it was not wise to ask for more details at that moment. I did not know that Maria and her family had received an eviction notice due to their inability to pay the rent. They were about three months behind. This prayer was their last hope of any relief or solution.

I asked her to share her last prayer request so we could begin the prayer. I was already in tears and ready to pray when Maria Elena began to cry. Through her tears she was able to ask for prayer for her husband.

"Pray for my husband," she said. "I love him, and he is a good man, but I have tried everything and don't know what else to do. He is sick and needs help. Maybe if you pray, God will make a difference in his life."

I could sense her desperation. Again, I was humbled and determined to pray. So we joined hands, and I prayed a desperate prayer to the Lord of heaven and earth. I ended the prayer by praying in the "powerful name of Jesus, our Redeemer" and said, "Amen." That prayer ended our visit, or so I thought. We said our goodbyes, traded hugs, and headed out the gate of their home and down the hill to the van to travel back to our hotel.

As we headed down the path to our van, the staff began to gather more information about Maria Elena's situation. Debbie and Dana asked for a debriefing and for gaps in the information they had received. As the details came in, I learned about the eviction and shared this with Debbie and Dana.

Debbie turned to me and said, "We have to do something about this, like now."

I asked the staff to explore the situation. During the two-hour ride back to the hotel, Debbie and Dana began asking questions. They asked how much it would take to buy a small plot of land for them to own? What would it take to build a home? How soon could we get started? The kingdom was coming near. The amazing part of this story is that Maria Elena's family had no idea this conversation was happening. Hope is often behind the scenes being worked out in ways we cannot imagine.

The staff did the research and came up with a figure of $6,000 to buy land and build a home for this family. We also learned that Oscar had been abusing his daughters, and the local magistrate had ordered him to go to jail to face charges of child abuse or to enter an alcohol rehabilitation program the day we left. The men of the local church gathered around Oscar and convinced him to go to rehab, and they made a commitment to support him throughout the program. Debbie and Dana went to work immediately on raising funds to build a home. The visit to Dulce's home was on a Thursday.

On Friday we caught our flights back to Dallas. By Sunday, I received a call from Debbie indicating that she and Dana had raised the $6,000 needed to get started. I sent word to our staff to begin looking for land for this family upon which to build a home. The kingdom of God came very near for this family.

About a year later, after mudslides damaged the new home construction, we continued construction, and with the support of a local church in the US, the family had their new home. Our team went to visit Maria Elena to dedicate their home and cut the ribbon. Oscar had gone through rehab and was there with the family, front and center. The girls were happy; Maria Elena's prayers were answered. We knew we could get them a new home, but we did not expect for them to also receive a new dad.

During that year since the day we met Oscar, he went through a year of rehab, counseling, and healing. The men of the church shared the gospel with Oscar, and he prayed to receive Christ. He went through a period of discipleship and was baptized publicly. The kingdom of God came near for this family. The family began to heal; Oscar was restored and healed. Their family relationships began to heal, and they had a new start with a new home. We saw peace, healing, and justice at work in this family because the kingdom came near. We keep in touch with Dulce, her sisters, Maria Elena, and Oscar. The family continues to thrive and grow. I asked the staff how Oscar was doing. They promptly reported that he was at work, earning a living for his family. My thought was that is where he should be. He has been restored to his rightful self. Jesus did this work in his life. We were only the instruments He used. Debbie and Dana were kingdom activators as well. In their hearts the matter was settled. They had to do what was right for this family. They felt led to raise funds to establish a permanent home for Dulce and her family. The King has come near to Oscar, to his family, to his wife and daughters.

This is what Buckner does: We bring the kingdom and all its benefits near. We follow the teachings of Jesus when He said, "Let the little children come to me, and do not hinder them, for the kingdom of heaven belongs to such as these" (Matthew 19:14). We follow the teachings of James, the half-brother of Jesus who said, "Religion that God our Father accepts as pure and faultless is this: to look after orphans and widows in their distress and to keep oneself from being polluted by the world" (James 1:27). We share the gospel, and we show the gospel in action. When we show up, the kingdom shows up too. We pray, "Your kingdom come, your will be done, on earth as it is in heaven" (Matthew 6:10). We expect our King to bring His kingdom near when we pray as He taught His disciples. Do you expect the kingdom to come near you and your church?

The Kingdom Near Your Church

Does your church bring the kingdom near? Dr. Boyd Hunt, my seminary professor, led a doctoral seminar on ecclesiology, the study of the church. He was writing a book at the time and used the manuscript of his book as the text for his course. The week before each doctoral seminar, he handed us a new chapter to read for class preparation. I will never forget the concepts he was testing out on us. He invited critique and feedback not only on the manuscript in terms of technical aspects but on the content as well. I recall him saying a few one-liners that have remained etched in my mind to this day. He said, "The church is the sign and agent of the kingdom of God." He was careful to point out that the church was not the kingdom. The kingdom was the kingdom. He said, "The church is at the cutting edge of redemptive history, at the edge of redemptive reality." He taught me the meta-narrative, the big story of the Bible as God's activity to redeem the world back to Him. He emphasized the reality of the kingdom now and yet to be. This helped me develop a framework for the local church, its purpose, and its mission as the sign of the kingdom present and the agent of the kingdom coming.

Dr. Hunt wrote, "The main idea of the church is this: *The people of God, redeemed or called out for a special purpose.* The focus is on a living reality, not on a building, an organization, or a place. Through the proclamation of the gospel of Jesus Christ, God is calling out a new covenant people to further His redemptive purposes throughout the world."[125] Hunt's vision of the church and his theology of the church in terms of redemptive history captured my imagination and heart. The church is not a building, an organization, or even a place. It is a people, the people of God. The church is the people of God called out of darkness into His wonderful light for a divine purpose in redemptive history. When you think of your church, is this what you imagine?

Is your church the sign of the kingdom? Do people experience the kingdom when they experience your church? Do the ministries of your church have enough room and space for people seeking hope, peace, healing, and justice? Is your church over-focused on internal activity at the expense of external engagement with people not yet a part of the family of faith? Does your church balance reaching in with reaching out? Does your church have a healthy balance between evangelism and social ministry? Is your church actively bringing the kingdom near for people outside the family of faith? Is your church the agent of the kingdom? Do you see your church as an active agent of the kingdom of God? Does your church budget reflect an outward focus on the community at large as well as an inward focus for its members? In what ways is your local church acting on behalf of the kingdom, bringing peace, healing, justice, and hope to people in your

---

[125] Boyd Hunt, *Redeemed!*, 173.

circle of influence? Does your church equip and engage you to act as an agent of the kingdom in your circle of family, neighbors, coworkers, and friends? Becoming a disciple who leads others to become disciples of Jesus is a great first step. Disciples who live as kingdom agents bring the kingdom near for those around them and bring hope, peace, healing, and justice for children, families, and communities.

Is your church at the cutting edge of redemptive history? I believe Dr. Hunt was right. The local church is the cutting edge of redemptive history. Samuel and Sugden argue that God's intention from the beginning is the final consummation of the kingdom, so the question becomes what to do between now and then. They contend that God's desire is His rule over the cosmos, not just the church or the nations and human society.[126] The local church makes history in heaven every time a sinner opens his or her heart and invites Jesus to come and become King. Churches make redemptive history when they teach, train, and disciple new believers in how to do everything Jesus taught. Churches make redemptive history when they engage and equip disciples to bring the kingdom near, redeeming all that has been damaged in their lives by bringing the power and presence of Jesus into difficult situations. Is your church at the cutting edge, making all things new for people who need hope?

The Kingdom Near the Wider Community of Jesus

Hunt wrote these words in the preface of his book, which he handed out in our doctoral seminar: "At the heart of God's eternal purposes through Christ and His kingdom . . . stand evangelism and missions, education, and social action."[127] Hunt saw these ministries as critical

---

[126] Vinay Samuel and Chris Sugden, "God's Intention for the World," *The Church in Response to Human Need,* eds. Vinay Samuel and Chris Sugden (Oxford: Regnum Books and William B. Eerdmans Publishing Company, 1987), 128–138.

[127] Hunt, *Redeemed!,* 11.

activities of the kingdom of God now. The kingdom of God is much larger than your local church. The kingdom is bigger than all institutions of Christian higher education put together. The kingdom is larger than all human welfare institutions put together. Ministries like Buckner International, World Vision, Compassion International, The Salvation Army, and many others like them are not together the kingdom. They are only a glimpse of the kingdom. They are only kingdom agents at the cutting edge. The kingdom is much larger, much more comprehensive, and much more brilliant than any one church, ministry, faith-based nonprofit, or Christian university.

Christian denominations are not the kingdom either. Presbyterians, Lutherans, Episcopalians, Anglicans, Baptists, Mennonites, Methodists, Assemblies of God, Pentecostals, church networks, and the like are not the kingdom either. Denominations that fly the flag of Jesus, preach and teach the Scripture, make and engage disciples, and live out the Christian life are part of the kingdom but not the kingdom in total.

I grew up within the framework of Texas Baptists, also known as the Baptist General Convention of Texas. Buckner International is an affiliated ministry of Texas Baptists. We find our connection with Texas Baptists in the Constitution of the Baptist General Convention of Texas, which says (italics mine): "The object of this Convention shall be to awaken and stimulate among the churches the greatest possible activity in evangelism, missions, Christian education and benevolent work and enterprises; to cultivate a closer cooperation among the churches and promote harmony of feeling and concert of action in *advancing all the interests of the Redeemer's kingdom.*"[128] Texas Baptists do not have a corner on the market of the kingdom, but

---

[128] "Constitution of the Baptist General Convention of Texas," Article II—Object, Downloads, Texas Baptists, accessed February 11, 2019, https://s3.amazonaws.com/texasbaptists/about/Constitution-adopted-by -BGCT-in -session+11-10-15.pdf.

through Buckner International and other sister agencies, universities, ministries, and churches, we envision advancing all the interests of the Redeemer's kingdom. This means we must not seek our own interests over that of our King. Ideally, there would be harmony in that priority and those of our ministries. The best mentors and coaches I have been blessed with have consistently encouraged me to seek the kingdom first as I lead in ministry, especially in the larger community of Jesus. My hope is that Christian pastors, leaders of denominations, agencies, universities, Bible colleges, seminaries, and faith-based ministries would see a vision for kingdom collaboration and unity where it makes kingdom sense for the King and all the interests of the Redeemer's kingdom.

People need hope now. They long for authentic possibilities and solutions that bring hope into their world. They generally care less about the label of your denomination or the name of your church, ministry, or university. People who are hurting can spot real hope in a minute from a mile away. They can also spot counterfeits and fake ministries, churches, and Christian institutions. False hope can be damaging and extremely harmful. People who experience a false sense of hope are plunged into deeper levels of hurt and pain resulting in total rejection of a God who loves them. What people want is hope, real hope, and they want it now. The kingdom is looking for agents willing to go to the cutting edge of redemptive history. The King is looking for messengers who will faithfully carry the message of redemption with courage right into the mess where people live and struggle to give a word of hope, peace, healing, and justice. Are you up to the task? Are you willing to go to the front lines of the battle over the precious lives of vulnerable children, orphans, families, and people who are desperate for a better life? The opportunity to make an eternal impact may be closer than you realize.

Questions to Consider

What does it mean to bring the kingdom near?

How does your church bring the kingdom near to its community?

How can your church be the sign and agent of the kingdom?

How might you bring the kingdom near to your circle of influence?

Why don't more Christian institutions engage in kingdom collaboration?

Chapter 9

HOPE SHINING ON VULNERABLE CHILDREN, ORPHANS, AND THEIR FAMILIES

A father of the fatherless, a defender of the widows, is God in his holy dwelling. God sets the lonely in families; he leads out the prisoners with singing.

—Psalm 68:5–6

Tom Davis, in his book *Fields of the Fatherless*, raised a biblical principle that should be prominent in our thinking as kingdom agents. He said, "The Holy Scripture is replete with references to three groups of people mentioned about 60 times: orphans, widows, and aliens (strangers). What they have in common is that they need provision and protection."[129] This is exactly the focus of the work of Buckner International. This is our story. This is our history. For the last 140 years, Buckner International has served vulnerable children, orphans, families, and seniors. I serve as the sixth president and chief executive officer of this marvelous ministry. In this role I have opportunities to speak on issues related to vulnerable children, orphans, and families.

On November 7, 2014, I was invited to speak at Harvard University during a conference hosted by Both Ends Believing, a

---

[129] Tom Davis, *Fields of the Fatherless: Discover the Joy of Compassionate Living* (Princeville, OR: Global Publishing Services, 2002), 25.

nonprofit organization and global working group dedicated to every child's human right to a permanent, loving family.[130] I flew into Boston and caught a taxi to the faculty building on campus where I was greeted by two Buckner leaders who were already at the conference as participants. The goal of the conference was to bring together about fifty leaders from developing countries to hear about best practices in child welfare. I was one of two guest speakers. As soon as I walked onto the campus, I was informed the schedule was running ahead of the plans and was asked if I was ready to walk up and present. I arrived in plenty of time to settle in, catch my breath, and hear other speakers, but now the plans changed. I was next in line to speak. I was ready.

My presentation was "Not One Orphan Child . . . But All Orphan Children: A Global Symposium on Achieving Child Permanency through Innovation." My assignment was to speak to the best practices of Buckner in global permanency. I have learned that one of the most important success factors of excellent speakers is to learn as much as possible about the audience and plan content that would make a positive impact on them. I learned that representatives from about seven countries were in the room who were leaders at the highest level of government responsible for child welfare. In many of the countries represented, child welfare services and systems were in early stages of development and far from the sophisticated systems and processes in the United States, as imperfect as our systems may be. The religious backgrounds of the participants included Muslim, Hindu, Buddhist, and Judeo-Christian worldviews. Several languages were spoken, so the conference was equipped with four translators stationed at the back of the hall simultaneously translating all presentations.

---

[130] I serve on the board of Both Ends Believing. For more information you can find them at www.bothendsbelieving.org.

The conferees were interested in best practices and how we did our work. I was prepared to share that information but also wanted to present what we did and why we did it from a philosophical perspective, so they would understand the foundations of our work and the level of excellence we deliver.

I came across a theoretical framework of reference developed by Thom Wolf called the WV3 Geo Lifezones Theory.[131] The framework is helpful in mapping or understanding global cultures and contexts. The premise is that every culture has a root luminary, a prototypical leader, spiritual mentor, and a voice that is adored by the people of that culture. This prototypical leader represents the roots of the culture. The leader develops a set of reflective lenses and perceptions, a systemic view, a mindset analysis, and the way people of that culture view life and reality. These are the shoots of the culture. Finally, the root luminary (who the culture adores) develops a reflective lens (how the culture analyzes) and lifestyle practices (how the culture acts or behaves). The lifestyle practices become the fruits, the social venue of mazeway actions (how the culture acts or behaves). The presentation of this model gave the group a way of conceptualizing global cultures in ways that are easily understood. The model uses a tree as a metaphor.

---

[131] Thom Wolf, "WV3: Worldvoice, Worldview, Worldvenue—the Voice-Venue Lifezones of the Planet," in *Social Change and Development: A Research Template*, ed. University Institute (New Delhi: University Institute, 2014).

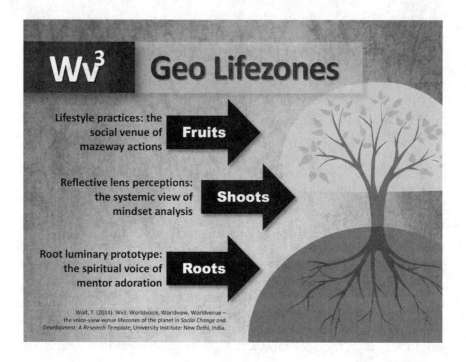

This model was very helpful since trees are a universal agricultural feature. Dr. Wolf and I took the WV3 Geo Lifezones framework and developed *The Buckner Orphan Tree*. Use of the tree metaphor with the application of roots, shoots, and fruits from a Buckner International perspective helped the participants better understand our perspective. The roots represented the orphan voice of our luminary, our prototypical leader, Jesus of Nazareth. The shoots represented the orphan view (how we view orphans) as represented by James, the half-brother of Jesus in the first century, and our founder, Dr. Robert Cooke Buckner, who imitated the view of James in the nineteenth century. The fruits represented the orphan venue and in practical terms, *children in families*.

My main message to the group was that we have come to believe the best place for children to grow and develop is in a healthy and safe family. This is where children learn who they are, are loved, cared for, nurtured, grow and develop. Given this philosophical view, Buckner has transitioned over the years from an orphanage in Dallas to providing services for foster care, adoption, single parents, and family strengthening to keep families together. We have learned that children in institutional care settings like orphanages ages birth through five years do not develop at the pace of their non-institutionalized peers. Children in that setting will lose one month of linear growth for every three months they are in institutional care.[132] We believe an orphanage is better than children living on

---

[132] Dawn Davenport, "Choosing Adoption—Developmental Impacts of Orphanages Versus Foster Care," accessed February 11, 2019, https://www.comeunity.com /adoption/health/adoption-orphanage-development.html.

the street; living in foster care is better than living in an orphanage; living in kinship care, a next of kin, may be preferable over foster care; returning a child to their family of origin in family reunification, if it is a healthy and safe environment, may be better than kinship care; and if none of these options is available, permanent adoption into a forever family is the best place for a child to grow and develop.

This message was strongly and affirmatively received. I recall one government representative who came to me to say, "I want you to come to Nepal to share *The Orphan Tree* with our government leaders, and when you come you will stay in my home as my personal guest."

"So you would want me to share my presentation and talk about how Jesus is the root of the Buckner Orphan Tree and why we do what we do?" I responded.

"Yes, I am a Muslim, and I would love for you to come to show us how Jesus teaches to take care of children," he said. "He is a good example for us."

During my tenure at Buckner, I have been very clear about the fact that we follow the teachings of Jesus of Nazareth in all the work we do. I am careful to add that we accept invitations to other countries not to proselytize but to serve vulnerable children, orphans, and families as guests of the government. I explain we may call on American volunteers to come and serve, volunteer their time, and even donate financially,. If they are asked why they came, they will also refer to Jesus as their leader and example. I usually add that if this is not the kind of engagement they would accept, Buckner may not be a good fit for their country. In every case I have received a warm welcome and have been encouraged to come with not a single exception.

The numbers of orphans in the world is staggering. The number of children who have lost both parents hovers around 17 million. The number of children worldwide who have lost either one parent or both parents is 150 million.[133] In the US there are more than 400,000 children in out-of-home care, and more than 100,000 are eligible for adoption in a forever family. In Texas, my home state, there are 32,000 children in out-of-home care, and 16,000 of them were in foster care for 2018. I wonder how we can bring the kingdom near to vulnerable children, orphans, and families in our midst. If they are on God's heart, should they not be on ours? What would our king want us to do in response to the needs of these children? Nothing will change unless we activate ourselves as agents of redemption, agents of the kingdom to bring the kingdom near. Speaking of nearness, we may find vulnerable children, orphans, and families are closer than we may think. They are in our communities, our cities, our state, our nation, and our world. They are also coming to us in large numbers. What must be our response?

Hope for Vulnerable Children at Home and in the Borderlands

Over the twelve years I have served at Buckner, we have seen several surges of children and families come to our southern border. But who could have ever predicted multiple caravans of people with thousands of people leaving their homes to journey toward Texas? The images you see in the news may cause a wide variety of reactions or sentiments. I know our donors and perhaps some of you reading this book have called to ask what Buckner was doing in response or what we should do. I wrote an opinion editorial piece to express our voice regarding this situation. My main message was that we serve vulnerable children and families on both sides of the border. In fact in 2017 we measured that Buckner impacted the lives

---

[133] "On Understanding Orphan Statistics," Christian Alliance for Orphans White Paper, accessed February 11, 2019, https://cafo.org/wp-content/uploads/2015/10/Orphan-Statistics-Web-9-2015.pdf.

of 23,925 children and adults in Guatemala, 4,694 in Honduras, and 31,575 in Mexico. For instance 260 adults received counseling services through our Buckner Family Hope Center in Jocotenango, Guatemala, while 160 adults and teens received vocational training through our new Family Hope Center in San José Pinula, Guatemala City, Guatemala. These families reside in the Northern Triangle at the intersection of Guatemala, Honduras, and El Salvador. Many people pass through the Northern Triangle to make their way to the United States.

Paul Collier, in his book *Exodus: How Migration Is Changing Our World*,[134] studied the people who migrate, the impact on the communities they leave behind, and the host societies who receive them. One of the points he makes is that migration is a global phenomenon not limited to the US-Mexico border but is impacting nation-states around the world. He argues that people leave their homeland to survive and to seek a better place to live.

The question will continue to surface for us: What will be the Buckner response? I don't think this issue is going away in our lifetime, and I don't think the question will diminish either. You may be asked this question as well: What is Buckner doing about the people coming to our borders?

Mexico Tenth Anniversary

I found an answer to this question on my last trip to Oaxaca, Mexico, to celebrate the tenth anniversary of Buckner Mexico. The staff prepared a wonderful time of celebration of our work. We visited a greenhouse project, a poultry enterprise, and a water purification and distribution project in one of the poorest communities in Oaxaca. I led a small contingency of Buckner leaders and a major

---

[134] Paul Collier, *Exodus: How Migration Is Changing Our World* (New York: Oxford University Press, 2013).

donor, Steven, a business owner in Dallas-Fort Worth. We drove to a community called Santa Ana Zegache. When our caravan pulled up, we were met by a delegation of community leaders, mostly women, who were working these projects. We met at the entrance of a property where the greenhouse project was being conducted. As we approached the group of about thirty people, a lone figure emerged as the leader of this community.

Her name was Aida, and she had started engaging with Buckner in January 2018. Though she could not be taller than four-and-a-half feet, she stood tall and proud. There was something about her; you could tell this lady was in charge. She came to the front of the group to greet us. A translator was set to translate her words for the group. Juan Carlos Millan, the executive director for Buckner Mexico, introduced her and gave her an opportunity to speak. She may have thought, "This is my only chance to get all my words said," so she started talking and went on, almost without taking a breath, and kept talking. The translator tried to interrupt so he could say what he remembered, but she took off and never looked back.

She said a lot of things as you would imagine. But at the very end of her speech, she said something that has stuck with me to this day. She said these words in Spanish: "I want to thank you on behalf of the families of this community for investing in us here in Zegache. I want you to know we are not afraid to work, and we are working your investment to produce vegetables, meat, and water for our children and our families. You have brought life and hope to our community. You have created work and opportunity for us, a gift we can never repay. We want you to know we now have work, and we are working in this community, so our husbands don't have to go to the north to find work, to suffer and to work for our survival. We want our men to come back to their families, to help us with this work. Our men have heard there is work here, and they are returning. Again, thank you for helping our lives change, for giving us a chance to work, and for helping us take care of our children and families."

Aida's words touched my heart. She spoke with passion, energy, and the conviction of a leader. It hit me like a ton of bricks. You may have already formed your opinion about what you see on the news regarding the US border with Mexico. As a US citizen you may be bothered, maybe annoyed, by the audacity of the folks who are coming to our border. I imagine we have a wide variety of views on immigration and political perspectives. All would agree that the rule of law is a foundational principle for the US. Crossing the US-Mexico borders without proper documents is illegal. Undocumented immigrants are required to follow due process under the law for entering the US or face paying fines, penalties, or deportation. I would expect this to be true of most if not all nations on the planet. Given these facts, I am reminded we all hold dual citizenship. We are citizens of the US, and we are also citizens of the kingdom of God—the kingdom Jesus said we should seek. When I see these people movements, I wonder what the Lord of redemptive history is doing and what He would have us do in response to children and families who suffer. Buckner is serving vulnerable families on both sides of the border. We serve families wherever we find them. We bring concrete solutions to strengthen families where they are. We find families in Oaxaca, in the Northern Triangle, at Reed Road in Houston, and at Bachman Lake in Dallas, and we are taking care of kingdom business.

We are keeping families together. We are making a way to reunite families. We are providing opportunities, work, and real solutions for families to survive and thrive. We are getting this done in Kenya, Peru, the Northern Triangle, the Dominican Republic, Mexico, and Texas.

We provide foster care and adoption in other countries, if we must. But we are also working hard to keep children in the families where God put them to start with. We call it family strengthening. It is a kingdom work. It is an awesome work. We are at the cutting edge of redemptive history. We are taking what was intended for harm and turning it into good. We are bringing the kingdom near.

The next time you see another news report about the negative consequences of migration caravans, remember your dual citizenship in this country and in the kingdom. Remember your King and His kingdom that we are to seek first, and remember there is a four-and-a-half-foot-tall community leader in Oaxaca, Mexico, who is deeply grateful for helping her family thrive right where they are. Remember her vision of men and fathers returning to them to be a family again. If you give her a chance to speak, she may try to say all that is on her mind, all that is on her heart, and all that is in her imagination about the hope we are shining brightly into her life.

Hope for Orphans in the Global Village

Inter-country adoptions to the US reached an apex in 2004 with about 23,000 placements. However, the trend has been downward recently reaching about 4,700 in 2017.[135] Globally, we are seeing a growing sentiment of nationalism and a reluctance for developing countries to allow inter-country adoption out of their countries to the United States. The exception seems to be for orphans with special needs. For many children the opportunity for inter-country placement remains the best alternative for a productive and healthy life. The declining trend in inter-country adoption

---

[135] "Adoption Statistics," Adoption Refererence, Intercountry Adoption, U. S. Department of State—Bureau of Consular Affairs, accessed June 26, 2019, https://travel.state.gov/content/travel/en/Intercountry-Adoption/adopt_ref /adoption-statistics.html.

allows orphans to stay in their culture, country, and community of origin. Buckner International decided to eliminate our program of inter-country adoptions due to this trend and instead developed a collaborative agreement with agencies who continue to place children internationally. We have shifted our resources and expertise to enhance capacity in developing countries to help government develop placement of children through foster care and adoption in those countries of origin.

One of the initiatives we have developed to remain at the cutting edge of these trends is to emphasize global permanency for foster care and adoption domestically in the countries where we serve. One of the places where hope shines brightly is in Kenya. Our team, led by Debbie Wynne, invests time and training in domestic adoption in Kenya resulting in seventy-eight placements on a budget of $67,000. In February 2018 I had the privilege of visiting many of these families firsthand to see the outstanding work being done.

I remember meeting Pauline in Kenya and learning about the embarrassment Pauline's mother felt the first time Pauline visited with her newly adopted daughter, Samantha. Pauline's mom didn't want her to take Samantha out. She was afraid of what the neighbors would say. But Pauline kept telling her mother they had to be confident and know she had done the right thing. The lesson for Pauline and her mom was that adoption is OK. The concept of adoption is not a normal practice in Kenyan culture. Pauline came to believe that adoption is divine, and there's a reason why God gives you a certain child. Today Samantha is such a part of Pauline's life sometimes Pauline doesn't remember she's adopted. Samantha is everything to Pauline. She's everything Pauline prayed for. Pauline's story is just one of many examples of how domestic adoption is becoming a trend in Kenya. Samantha has a family because Pauline was willing to go to the frontline to bring the kingdom near for one little girl.

Hope for Families as the Core of Society

The family is the core of society. From the very beginning of human history, God established a father and a mother to bring children into the world to protect, love, nurture, and provide for their flourishing. That is not to say any family is perfect. All families are under construction and in need of improvement from the impact of the fall in Genesis. The story line is evident throughout the witness of Scripture. Where the family has broken down, our goal is to rebuild the family toward a healthy place. Samuel and Samuel contend that the vision for the family in the Bible is to reconcile families and attempt to bring wholeness of relations to the whole community as the family of families.[136] Families are reconciled through the power and presence of Christ in their lives. Christ is Lord of our families. He leads, provides, blesses, forgives, and corrects. It is through this hard work that parents and children learn how to get along because they are properly related to God through Christ.[137]

My work with Buckner has proven that poor families have resources they need to share in community building. They do not participate resourceless.[138] I have seen this reality in Buckner Family Hope Centers in the US and in developing countries. Our focus is to work with poor families to strengthen them using existing resources. Vinay and Colleen Samuel agree that "Evangelicals . . . saw families as the basic unit among the urban poor. They inevitably responded to the needs of women and children and enabled men to learn responsibility. This approach stressed economic support and marital fidelity while seeking to restore the breadwinner to the home, and protected women and children from the ravages of male desertion

---

[136] Vinay Samuel and Colleen Samuel, "Rebuilding Families: A Priority for Wholistic Mission," in *Transformation*, Vol. 10, No. 3, July 1993, p. 5–7.

[137] Ibid.

[138] Ibid.

and violence."[139] I have seen families healed and restored repeatedly during my tenure at Buckner. It is a joy to see men and women learn parenting skills, how to bless their children, and how to develop a healthy environment for their children. Fathers and mothers turn their hearts and homes toward their children when they have the support, training, and encouragement needed.

In 2008 leaders at Buckner International began to raise questions about the possibility of reaching out to families before they reached out to us for help. They began asking, "What if we were able to work with families who were struggling, perhaps on the brink of collapse, and strengthen them before the abuse, abandonment, or neglect begins? What if we could intervene with strategies that helped families get stronger and become successful? What if we could prevent children from coming into the system of child welfare to begin with?"

We began to develop a model, and with the help of a very generous donor, we implemented the program in Guatemala and referred to these centers as Community Transformation Centers. Randy Daniels was the lead implementer of this model, and he rapidly deployed resources given to us, developed the model, and began staffing. We saw this model expand in other cities in Guatemala, then in Honduras, and ultimately across our system. We wondered if this model would work in Texas and imported the approach back to the US. It worked perfectly in the South Texas Valley and then at all other locations in Texas. After reflecting on our success, I realized we were not transforming the community but were bringing hope to families. We changed the name from Community Transformation Centers to Family Hope Centers. In Family Hope Centers, we offer customized solutions to families struggling with deep issues so

---

[139] Ibid.

they can become independent, strong, and healthy. We really don't transform a community; rather, we provide hope to families. Over time as we are successful and families gain strength, the community is transformed.

Our Family Hope Center in Peñitas, Texas, is a shining example of how we provide hope to struggling families. Several years ago, Ricardo Brambila was serving near McAllen, Texas, in a community called Peñitas. He told me about a couple with three children living together in a common law marriage. I will call them Jose and Maria. Jose came to us asking for financial support to pay the utility bill. He had announced to Maria that he was leaving her but wanted to get the bill paid and not leave her with a debt. We agreed to provide support but asked if they were willing to enter the Family Hope Center program through family coaching to determine how they came to the point of needing help, so we could attack the root problem. They agreed. We immediately set goals and priorities for the next ninety days. After they completed their first segment of coaching and celebrated their victories, we asked the couple what they wanted to set as priorities for the second ninety days.

Jose turned toward Maria and said, "I want to marry her."

"What?" Maria said. "I thought you were leaving me."

"No, I am not leaving," Jose answered. "I want to marry you."

So they asked if we could help them get married, and we agreed. I inquired of Jose and asked our staff what we did to make such a dramatic difference in this family. They said we enrolled Jose in a training program in landscaping because he enjoyed that kind of work. Jose was hired by a company and within ninety days was promoted to supervisor of a landscaping crew. When he came to the second ninety-day planning session, he had training, a job, and a promotion. He said he did not think he was qualified to be a father or a husband because he could not provide for his family. He felt it was better to leave than to face the shame of not providing for his family. Once we solved that problem, the family had a fighting chance.

As Ricardo Brambila continued to work with couples like Jose and Maria, he found many were in common law marriages but wanted to formalize their commitments to each other. One day Ricardo called me and asked, "How would you like to help me officiate a mass marriage of twelve couples who want to get married?"

"If you do the counseling, I will come to help you officiate the wedding for these couples," I said.

It was a wonderful experience to officiate the wedding of twelve couples in one ceremony. When word got out to other Buckner leaders that we were conducting a mass wedding, there was some pushback on the idea.

"Does Buckner do weddings now?" they asked.

"We serve families," I answered. "And if a wedding is what they need, we will do all we can to deliver solutions."

Ricardo and I happen to be licensed and ordained ministers, so these weddings were legal and official. As I reflected, I began to think there is no better way to secure a future for the children of these couples than to encourage lifelong commitment through a wedding ceremony of parents who love each other. A simple wedding ceremony does not guarantee lifelong marriages, but I also know you can't finish well unless you start. Having been married thirty-seven years, I know marriage is hard work that requires a love commitment, determination, and the presence of the Lord in our lives to succeed. I know some marriages fragment even with the best intentions. That is why we have programs for single parents to succeed and raise healthy and happy children. I also believe children deserve loving parents who do their best to provide a healthy and safe environment in which to grow and mature into adulthood. This is what Buckner is all about. We believe the family is the core of society. But to raise healthy and thriving families, we need help. *We need your help*. Have you considered how you might deliver solutions and resources to serve vulnerable children, orphans, and families in the global village, in your state, in your community? How does your life assignment connect to bringing the kingdom near? Keep reading.

Questions to Consider

What is God's heart for the fatherless?

How might you respond to the number of orphans in the world?

Do the number of children in foster care and potential adoptions surprise you?

What is the kingdom response to vulnerable children, orphans, and families at our borders?

What would you and your church be willing to do to help serve struggling families so their children can stay in their home of origin?

Chapter 10

HOPE: PEACE, HEALING, AND JUSTICE AS YOUR KINGDOM ASSIGNMENT

So be very careful how you live. Do not live like those who are not wise, but live wisely. Use every chance you have for doing good, because these are evil times. So do not be foolish but learn what the Lord wants you to do.

—Ephesians 5:15–17 NCV

Ephesians 5:15–17 are some of my favorite verses in the Bible. Paul, the apostle, called by Jesus on the road to Damascus and recruited by the Lord to serve Him, wrote these timeless words., making the point that we should be thoughtful, wise, and deliberate in the way we choose to live our lives. His words encourage wise living rather than foolish living due to the evil times in which we live. He set a standard of wise living and foolish living. Wise living requires learning what the Lord wants you to do with your life. It is learnable, not a mystery. The wise life can be learned. Foolish living would be to live a life without purpose and direction, without a sense of mission defined by your King and His kingdom. Have you learned what the Lord wants to do with your life? Have you discovered your life mission, life purpose? Is it tied to the mission of the king and His kingdom?

Your Kingdom Assignment

Several books have been written by Christian authors related to living a meaningful life. The most popular books include *The Purpose Driven Life* by Rick Warren and *Experiencing God* by Henry Blackaby. However, few books have been written and very little material has been produced to guide followers of Christ to measure their lives and the purpose they will pursue. I developed a tool called Destino: Leader Development Profile,[140] a personal and practical tool to help emerging leaders and followers of Christ crystallize their commitments and purpose and focus their energies, gifts, talents, abilities, experiences, and educational background into one cohesive life thrust. Destino is a guide to help individuals figure out the purpose of their lives in the context of a life profile resulting in a clearly articulate mission statement. This kind of laser focus is useful to discriminate between good, better, and best choices in life so that you can fulfill your God-given mission.

I first came across this system in the early 1990s when I attended a seminar at the Spare Not Missions Conference at The Church on Brady, currently known as MOSAIC, in Los Angeles, California. Thom Wolf was the senior pastor, and Carol Davis was the coordinator of this missions-activation event. I attended a seminar led by Robert Sowell entitled, "Developing a Life Mission Statement: When You Get to Where You Are Going, Where Will You Be?" I was intrigued by the title of the seminar and was looking for more definition in my life and ministry. I was about thirty-two years old at that time. Years later as I was reflecting on the literature of human development, I learned about the work of Daniel Levinson, a researcher at Yale University who formed a theory of personality

---

[140] For more information about using the LDP tool, email areyes@buckner.org or call 214-758-8190.

development. Levinson's theory is an evolving "life structure: the underlying pattern or design of a person's life at a given time."[141] The structure is built around whatever the person considers to be most important, such as people, places, things, institutions, and causes as well as values, dreams, and emotions. One of Levinson's stages is called the "culminating life structure for early adulthood." During this stage a person begins to make deeper commitments to work and family, to set timetables for specific life goals, to establish a niche in society, and to realize youthful aspirations. As I reflect upon that time, I can remember sensing the place in life that Levinson describes. I was open and searching for greater purpose and a way to simplify my purpose.

By the end of the ninety-minute session, I had written all over the paper Robert Sowell gave to us. After that conference I continued to reflect and write until I developed a life mission statement: *To develop kingdom leaders from my circle of influence to the ends of the earth.* I have continued to use this statement from the early 1990s through the current time. It has become a powerful tool to help me make significant life and career choices as well as decisions regarding the use of my time. This tool is not a vocational guide. It is much larger and expansive than that. Destino is a guide to help a Jesus follower choose his or her life purpose. A career is merely a means to an end in this model. This model helps emerging leaders find their passion, mission, and vision; decide on the results that are worth their life and connect those results to their leadership; determine significant relationships needed to advance this mission; specify life tasks and leadership goals; and blend these factors into one cohesive statement that can be used to navigate the stewardship of their lives.

---

[141] Daniel J. Levinson, "A Conception of Adult Development," Yale University, accessed February 12, 2019, https://pdfs.semanticscholar.org/5e75/2a77fb59cc 48e9eea4b1ef4c53056b0f140e.pdf.

Research shows that the best age to engage in this kind of reflection is between the ages of twenty-two and thirty-three. Levinson's Life Structure Theory[142] recommends several phases of life structure, the fashion in which a person structures his or her life. During the entry life structure for early adulthood, adults between the ages of twenty-eight and thirty-three find a dream and a mentor to help them structure their lives. During the age-thirty transition, adults twenty-eight to thrity-three reassess their work and family patterns and create the basis for the next life structure. That is not to say a person younger or older than ages twenty-two to thirty-three would not benefit from this type of planning and development. Levinson's theory seems to correlate to the most optimum time in the development of an adult to make lifetime commitments. For most adults this is a time when they are entering college, starting their families, and entering a career. It is imperative that followers of Christ take the time to reflect on one's life purpose at this stage of development. Personally, the second life marker that shaped my willingness to consider my life purpose was a near-death accident when I was twenty-two. I had an automobile accident that should have taken my life. I walked away from that experience wondering what my life purpose was, given that by all accounts my life should have ended at that time.

During the funeral service of the late 41st US President George H. W. Bush, his son, 43rd US President George W. Bush, recounted stories from his father's life, including the two times he nearly died. The first was as a teen from a staph infection. The second was during World War II. While on a bombing mission, President George H. W. Bush's plane was shot down over the Pacific Ocean. Two men on his crew lost their lives, but Navy Pilot George H. W. Bush was pulled

---

[142] Ibid.

from the ocean after floating on a life raft. The future president had prayed for rescue while on that raft. And as his son recounted at his funeral, "God answered those prayers, and turned out He had other plans for George H. W. Bush. . . . Those brushes with death made him cherish the gift of life, and he vowed to live every day to the fullest."

Facing the reality of death is usually not considered until later in life when senior adults begin to realize their lives are coming to an end. Papalia, Olds, and Fieldman[143] cite a study involving thirty-nine women whose average age was seventy-six. The study found that those who saw the most purpose in life had the least fear of death.

According to Elizabeth Kübler-Ross, facing the reality of death is a key to living a meaningful life. She says:

> It is the denial of death that is partially responsible for people living empty, purposeless lives; for when you live as if you'll live forever, it becomes too easy to postpone the things you know that you must do. . . . In contrast, when you fully understand that each day you awaken could be the last you have, you take the time that day to grow, to become more of who you really are, to reach out to other human beings.[144]

Think for a moment with the end in mind. Knowing you have limited days, how should you plan to use the time you have remaining to determine and complete your kingdom assignment? Finding your specific kingdom assignment and results provides for a scenario which will produce high life output and creative performance for the sake of the kingdom. Selecting your life results is another way

---

[143] Diane E. Papalia, Sally Wendkos Olds, and Ruth Duskin Feldman, *Human Development* (New York: McGraw Hill, 2001).

[144] Elizabeth Kübler-Ross, *Death: The Final Stage of Growth* (New York: Simon and Schuster, 1975), 164.

of saying no to many possibilities. The Apostle Paul had this kind of focus and said:

> Not that I have already obtained all this, or have already arrived at my goal, but I press on to take hold of that for which Christ Jesus took hold of me. Brothers and sister, I do not consider myself yet to have taken hold of it. But one thing I do: Forgetting what is behind and straining toward what is ahead, I press on toward the goal to win the prize for which God has called me heavenward in Christ Jesus. —Philippians 3:12–14

The Apostle Paul had a singular focus to live out the purpose for which Jesus selected him. He focused on one thing: to press toward the goal to win the prize for which he had been called. The good you might do becomes the enemy of better, and better is the enemy of the best. Light diffused is helpful, but focused light into the shape of a laser can cut steel and perform surgical procedures on the human body. A focused life tends to deliver the best results for the kingdom. This is the theme of Strategic Coach's Unique Ability Model,[145] which suggests everyone is incompetent at something; most are competent at fewer things; still fewer reach excellence in specific endeavors; and highly productive leaders reach maximum effectiveness when they are performing their unique ability. A unique ability is a superior skill performed as a matter of passion, producing energy with openness to constant improvement.

Unique ability is a set of habits and talents you may develop over your lifetime. Over time you may develop a skill set in many different situations. These activities are at the center of what gives you energy. You may be the most successful when you are combining talents with intelligence while applying this combination to what you

---

[145] Catherine Nomura, Dan Sullivan, Julia Waller, and Shannon Waller, *Unique Ability: Creating the Life You Want* (Toronto, Ontario: The Strategic Coach Inc., 2003).

really care about. Your unique ability includes passion, ease, growth, results, and impact. Passion means you cannot wait to get the day started to begin an endlessly stimulating and satisfying project. Ease suggests the activity flows without opposition. Growth suggests the more you have the opportunity to develop your unique ability, the more powerful it becomes. Impact means peers want to be around you because your unique ability generates energy they want to experience. This kind of leader influences people in a positive and creative way.[146] Once you decide on your kingdom results that are worth exchanging your life for and find your unique ability, you will establish purposeful relationships to do your kingdom assignment. Once you figure out what the Lord wants you to do and you focus your kingdom assignment, you will be in an enhanced position to use all you have to bring the kingdom near for people who need hope.

Hope and Your Kingdom Assignment

Your kingdom assignment is not only for you, the King, and His kingdom; it will most likely bring hope to people in your circle of influence. When you accomplish your kingdom assignment, you bring the kingdom near. You also bring hope, peace, healing, and justice with your assignment. As you align your kingdom assignment with seeking the kingdom first in all you do, you will see the impact of your life for redemptive history. Knowing you are living out your kingdom purpose, using your gifts, talents, experiences, training, personality, character, and wisdom to make an eternal difference gives meaning and a sense of fulfillment. I cannot recommend a better way to live, to explore, to create, or to imagine for something greater than you and beyond your lifetime. You may be a lawyer, an engineer, a business analyst, consultant, teacher, coach, financial

---

[146] Ibid., 6.

professional, business executive, a social worker, a nonprofit leader, a minister, or one of many occupations. I am convinced there must be more to life than surviving, paying bills, or even being successful financially. There must be more than accumulating wealth and living comfortably. To what end are you living if not for the kingdom?

In his book, *Business By Design*, Raymond Harris[147] unearths an expansive array of business principles from the parables of Jesus in the New Testament. Raymond is a friend and supporter of our work at Buckner International. This year I invited Raymond to be a guest speaker at our annual leadership retreat at Camp Buckner near the Texas Hill Country. The theme of our conference was growing leaders. The theme passage for the conference was 2 Timothy 2:1–7. In it, Paul instructed Timothy to select reliable men who are also qualified to teach others. Paul outlined three metaphors for Timothy to consider as paradigms for leadership: the solider, the athlete, and the farmer. Then in verse 7 he concludes by saying, "Reflect on what I am saying, for the Lord will give you insight into all this."

I took this framework and invited Raymond Harris as a business leader to share principles of leadership he learned in business and to share his new book. I invited Navy Commander Bryan Crittendon, who serves as a chaplain in Pensacola, Florida, to speak about leadership from a military perspective, and I invited Charean Williams, a sports writer and the first female selector for the Pro Football Hall of Fame, to reflect on leadership from the world of sports. I also invited Dr. Thom Wolf to set the biblical background for leadership from the Timothy passage. He called it *God's Triple A: Army, Athletics, and Agribusiness*. These speakers did an excellent job speaking from their areas of expertise. Raymond said something that stuck with me during that conference when he said, "The purpose

---

[147] Raymond Harris, *Business By Design: Applying God's Wisdom for True Success* (Savage, MN: BroadStreet Publishing, 2018).

of business is to create margin, but what is the purpose of margin?" He answered, "The purpose of creating margin is to bless and serve other people in need." He was aligning his life business and success with principles of the kingdom of God. After two years studying the parables of Jesus, Raymond narrowed the meaning of business down to creating margin, then using it to serve others. Raymond figured it out. Living for the King, pursuing all the interests of the Redeemer's kingdom, is the best way to live. Using your gifts, skills, abilities, and experiences as you seek the kingdom is the highest form of personal stewardship. Would you ever imagine your life would bring peace, healing, and justice to other people through your life mission?

Peace, Healing, and Justice and Your Kingdom Assignment

My hope is that reading the pages of this book may activate your imagination regarding the purpose of your life as it relates to the kingdom of God. Your imagination may entertain the notion you have a specific place in redemptive history, the history of God on the earth, for eternity. You may not have considered the possibility that God would bring peace to other people through your life. If the Prince of Peace lives in you, His peace is in you and goes with you. Wherever you go, your King goes with you. Since His peace lives in you, you bring a sense of peace to people in your circle of influence who need help. You bring peace to a vulnerable child, an orphan, or a family when you show up, when you pray, when you participate in their lives, when you train them, and when you give of your time, your talents, and your treasure. You bring the kingdom when you come near. You bring your skills, abilities, experiences, training, resources, and all that you have become to bear on being with people who are hurting, children who are wounded, families who need help.

You may not have considered the possibility that your presence in a person's life could bring a level of healing to a wounded child or a broken family. The God who heals lives within you. He desires to use your life as an instrument of healing. You bring healing when you get close enough to pray for a child, when you pray for parents, and when you pray for a hurting family. You bring healing with you when you provide a way for a child to have a place in a foster family. You bring healing when you provide a way for a child or orphan to be adopted into a forever family. You bring healing when you make a way for a struggling single mom or dad to be in a secure place where they can dream again, get an education, and find a way toward economic independence away from the people or things that put them in a tough situation. You bring healing when you put a pair of shoes on a child who needs shoes to go to school. You bring healing when you take the time to read to a child when that is not his or her normal experience. You bring healing when you take people who feel invisible and call them by their name. You bring healing with a smile or a hug. You bring healing when you activate your vocational experience to provide a level of expertise that a family needs for support and success. You bring healing in Jesus' name by contributing your time, your talent, and your treasure. You bring healing because Jehovah Rapha, the God who heals, lives in you.

You may not have considered you would be capable of bringing justice into the life of a vulnerable child, an orphan, or a family. When you show up to gather shoes or lead a shoe drive, you are making a just way to give a small gift to children and adults. When you financially support a Buckner program and allow us to use it wherever needed most, you provide a just way for our expert staff to apply needed resources to feed families, to equip families toward success, to place children in a foster family, to place a child in an adoptive family, to place a child in kinship care, and to work toward the reunification of that child back to his or her family. You bring a sense of justice from an economic perspective when you make a way for families to work, to provide food and clean water for their children. You provide a way for justice to exist when you support Buckner to change laws in developing countries so children have a right to a family rather than being placed in jail after an episode of sexual or physical abuse. You overturn injustice teens face when they age out of foster care only to face the prospect of drug addiction, prostitution, or gang membership by providing a way for after care programs that lead to independence and financial sustainability. You make justice happen when you bring the kingdom near.

In his book *The Hole in Our Gospel*, Richard Stearns, former president of World Vision, quoted President Jimmy Carter who once stated that the greatest problem facing our generation was the growing gap between the richest and poorest people on earth. Stearns pointed to the second greatest commandment that tells us to love our neighbors. He added the next crucial question: "Who is my neighbor?"[148] At the very beginning of his book, Stearns asked the question: What does God expect of us? He contends that being a Christian is much more than having a personal relationship with Christ but also having a public and transformational relationship with the world around us. The prophet Micah recorded an answer to the question of what God expects from us when he wrote: "He has showed you, O mortal, what is good. And what does the LORD require of you? To act justly and to love mercy and to walk humbly with your God" (Micah 6:8). The three requirements for a life well lived are to do justice, to love mercy, and to walk humbly. In practical terms you might say it this way: "Pull weeds, do deeds, and plant seeds." Pulling weeds is a thankless job but somebody must do it. When you encounter weeds that must be

---

[148] Richard Stearns, *The Hole in Our Gospel: The Answer That Changed My Life and Might Just Change the World* (Nashville: Thomas Nelson, 2009), 99.

pulled in your community, you bring hope and justice. When you do deeds because it is the right thing to do rather than what is deserved or merited, you bring hope and healing. When you plant seeds of the good news along the way, you bring hope and peace. Buckner is at its best when pulling weeds, doing deeds, and planting seeds.

Our starting point is in lives of vulnerable children, orphans, and families who need help and assistance. We address issues of injustice, and we love people through our actions, providing solutions to real-life problems. At the right moment, when people ask why we pull weeds and do deeds, we plant seeds of the love of Jesus. We address both sides of the coin. We provide solutions to immediate needs, and we answer questions about eternity through spiritual development activities like prayer, Bible study, and worship in a local church. We serve about four hundred thousand vulnerable children, orphans, families, and seniors annually. We routinely witness about one thousand people come to faith in Jesus Christ through our work as a natural outcome on an annual basis. We shine hope, offer peace, and bring healing and justice when we bring the kingdom near through our ministry. Our team members have their kingdom assignments, and they are on mission. They are passion-driven, Christlike, and servant leaders bringing the kingdom near every day.

Since Buckner is not a church, we need volunteers, followers of Jesus, to serve, to make disciples, and to offer fellowship. We need churches to augment our work by providing a community for those coming to faith in Christ. We plow the fields, plant seeds, and do deeds, but there is much more work that needs to be done as we bring the kingdom near. We can help you apply your kingdom assignment in places closer than you may realize. Are you prepared to go with us? Will you join us as you live out your kingdom assignment?

Questions to Consider

What is your kingdom assignment?

What is the purpose of your life?

What are ways you can live out your kingdom assignment while using your vocational skills and talents?

How might you bring hope, peace, healing and justice through your life?

Who is your neighbor?

GOOD WORDS, GOOD WORKS, AND GOOD WILL

I started this writing project in 2017 with a burr under my saddle as we say in Texas. It was a burden in my heart, perhaps an unreconciled reality about two teams: one focused on evangelism and the other focused on serving others. I learned and grew up on a split gospel—split between telling about the peace Jesus brings and showing the peace He brings along with healing and justice.

The Great Generation were builders. They built institutions, denominations, ministry agencies, churches, and ministries we still enjoy today. The generations before us launched the greatest missionary movement in human history, several great awakenings of the Spirit of God across our land, and many wonderful institutions of higher learning to train young ministers, future missionaries, and professionals to live out their chosen profession with biblical convictions and hearts trained on the redemptive movement of God in history. I personally benefited from training for ministry at Southwestern Baptist Theological Seminary where I received an incredibly helpful theological education for a life of ministry.

That was then. This is now. My generation has carried on the legacy of those that came before us and has achieved many wonderful things for the kingdom as well. In the 1960s and 1970s, the Jesus Movement attracted many young people toward the idea of simple living and countercultural ideas in reaction to the turbulent decades of the 1950s and 1960s. Movements like the Calvary Chapel movement grew out of this era. Explo '72 was an event organized by Campus Crusade for Christ with the involvement of conservative leaders like Bill Bright and evangelist Billy Graham. Other church movements like Hope Chapel Churches, Vineyard Churches, and many other para-church organizations grew out of this era. However, one of the unintended consequences of generations past was the development of a division between evangelism and ministry among the least of these. I came across a modern paraphrase of the passage of Matthew 25:42–43 developed by Richard Stearns, former president of World Vision. He wrote:

> For I was hungry, while you had all you needed. I was thirsty, but you drank bottled water. I was a stranger, and you wanted me deported. I needed clothes, but you needed *more clothes.* I was sick, and you pointed out the behaviors that led to my sickness. I was in prison, and you said I was getting what I deserved. (RESV—Richard E. Stearns Version)[149]

I grew up under the influence of the team of the gospel that focused on evangelism sometimes to the exclusion of everything else. I did not experience much emphasis on serving the needs of struggling people in our community. Richard Stearns's paraphrase of Matthew 25 hits home to me. I came to Buckner International in 2007 as president of the Buckner Children and Family Services division as part of a succession plan. I was to lead and serve this outstanding ministry serving vulnerable children, orphans, families, and seniors. I still had an evangelistic, church planting, missional perspective, but in this role I experienced a total immersion into the ministry of hurting children and families right here in Texas and in developing countries. My heart began to shift toward a balance between evangelism and ministry toward both sides of the gospel.

---

[149] Stearns, *The Hole in Our Gospel,* 59.

The Statement on Social Justice and the Gospel

Some leaders in evangelical Christianity, however, still struggle with the concept that evangelism and ministry are two sides of the same coin. In 2018 the Statement on Social Justice and the Gospel[150] was published online resulting from a meeting that took place on June 19, 2018. Fourteen men met at Herb's Coffee House in Dallas, Texas, to express their growing concern with much that was taking place within evangelical circles under the banner of social justice. After much discussion and several meetings, the group drafted fourteen articles containing affirmations and denials. The group did not claim any ecclesiastical authority but only issued the statement to call attention to and clarify various concerns. Some of the signers I recognize include John MacArthur, Voddie Baucham, and many others.

The statement includes strong affirmations and denials regarding Scripture, the Imago Dei (the image of God), justice, God's law, sin, the gospel, salvation, the church, heresy, sexuality and marriage, complementarianism, race and ethnicity, culture, and racism. For the most part, I find harmony in these affirmations and denials. However, there were a few affirmations and denials that caused me to reread, rethink, and reflect on my theological perspective regarding the message of this book.

The Gospel: Affirmations and Denials

When affirming the gospel, the writers of this statement narrowed the meaning of gospel to only the definition of who Jesus is regarding salvation or His work of being our Savior. The statement does not allow for the application or implication of the gospel such as living

---

[150] The Statement on Social Justice and the Gospel can be found at www.statementonsocialjustice.com, accessed Feburary 12, 2019.

justly in the world as definitional components of the gospel. While I agree with the definition of the gospel of this statement, I find it hard to separate the application and implication of our salvation as part of the gospel itself. The writers of this statement would separate the gospel message from gospel living. I see the point, but I don't see it in the life of Jesus as recorded in the New Testament. This is the very point I have been writing about in the preceding chapters. I would have expected some reflection in the article about the relationship of the gospel and the kingdom of God. Jesus spoke of the gospel and the kingdom when He said, "This gospel of the kingdom will be preached to the whole world as a testimony to all nations, and then the end will come" (Matthew 24:14). The "gospel of the kingdom" refers to the teachings of Jesus, all of them. The gospel is the message by which we learn we are sinners and need a Savior. This same Savior and message have ethical dimensions that must not be separated from its impact on daily life.

The Church: Affirmations and Denials

The article affirms that the primary role of the church is to worship through the preaching of His Word, teaching sound doctrine, observing baptism and the Lord's Supper, equipping the saints, and evangelizing the lost. The denial states that political and social activism should not be viewed as integral components of the gospel or primary to the mission of the church. The denial encourages using the laws of society to have some effect on society. The statement contends that this is not part of the central mission of the church. Once again, I see much harmony with the statement for the most part. However, it appears the statement suggests the church's mission is limited to the spiritual and transformational impact of the gospel message on the life of believers with little to no emphasis on society. While I agree the church does not have a political mission or a social activist mission, I have argued throughout this book the church's mission must include a redemptive and transformational impact on the poor, the vulnerable child, the orphan, and struggling families. Their definition of the church's mission seems too narrow given all I have studied, read, and reported in this book. I would have expected some reflection on the church and its role as the sign and agent of the kingdom of God. The Statement on Social Justice and the Gospel seems to be an attempt to correct mission-drift of the evangelical church. I understand the need for such a statement and the concerns it addresses.

An Open Letter to the Next Generation

Those who grew up in America during the Great Depression and World War II have become characterized as the "Greatest Generation." The Baby Boomers, who were born mostly following World War II and through the 1960s, live in the shadows of this great generation. Boomers were the largest generation in American history at the time and introduced the concept of mega-churches and seeker-sensitive and seeker-driven approaches to evangelism and church growth. The Boomers may soon be eclipsed by the Millennial generation (those born in the 1980s and 1990s) in terms of size and hopefully by kingdom impact. Our time is running out. The day will come when we pass the baton to the next generation of kingdom leaders. Generation X (born from the mid-to-early 1960 to 1980), Millennials, and Generation Z (born after the turn of the century) will carry the task of the two great commandments into the future. In fact it is already happening. Young professionals are flooding the marketplace and taking on positions of leadership.

My encouragement to the next generation is to take from the best of our past generations and create a new future as kingdom seekers who preach, teach, and show the gospel. But you must start with showing and back into preaching and teaching. You will have a better audience among those you are serving. People need hope now. Give it to them by providing real solutions, real answers that bring peace, healing, and justice into their lives now. Once they know how much you care, they will want to know why you care. Tell them about Jesus. Don't back off the King. Tell them who He is, what He did on the Cross, how much He loves them, and what He as our King commands us to do. Then tell them about Robert Cooke Buckner. In a day with so much opposition to the Christian message, dislike of Christian churches, and efforts to limit religious liberty and speech, people will not be able to refute the man and his message. It is our story. Tell it with confidence. To look forward, create, and dream a bright future, look back and discover our past. Go back to the future and you will find your way in the decades to come. It really is that simple.

Dr. Robert Cooke Buckner: The Man, His Message, and His Method[151]

Dr. Robert Cooke Buckner was a Baptist preacher from Madisonville, Tennessee. He began serving as a pastor at the age of seventeen. He was the son of a Baptist pastor and grandson of Baptist missionaries. He migrated to Texas with a stop in Albany, Kentucky, where he served as a pastor of the First Baptist Church. He met and married Vienna, and the two moved to Texas in 1859 on the eve of the Civil War. The more I study his life and work, the more impressed I am with him. He landed in Paris, Texas, to pastor the First Baptist Church there. For almost twenty years he served as pastor but also served the community and the state in which he lived.

---

[151] For a more thorough summary of the life and work of Robert Cooke Buckner, see my book *The Jesus Agenda: Becoming an Agent of Redemption* (Dallas: Believers Press, 2015), 65–74.

The year Dr. Buckner crossed the border into Texas, General Sam Houston was running for governor and was elected right before the Civil War. Years prior, General Houston fought valiantly to establish Texas's independence from Mexico and the Republic of Texas in 1836 and led the new republic to join the United States of America in 1845 after nine years as an independent nation. Fourteen years later, Dr. Buckner came on the scene to a new state. After Abraham Lincoln was elected president of the United States, Texas joined the Confederacy of the South, and General Houston was ousted from Texas government due to his support of remaining as one union and his anti-slavery sentiments. Dr. Bucker saw the collapse of thousands of frontier families whose fathers went to fight for the Confederacy and never returned. Children became orphans, and wives became widows by the thousands. Dr. Buckner saw families disintegrate and felt compelled to do something about it.

He was impacted by the verse of Scripture written by James, the half-brother of Jesus, "Religion that God our Father accepts as pure and faultless is this: to look after orphans and widows in their distress and to keep oneself from being polluted by the world" (James 1:27). He leveraged his contacts and relationships with Texas Baptists since he served for nineteen consecutive years as the president of the Baptist General Convention of Texas, and he published a newspaper called the *Religious Messenger*, which he distributed for profit through a printing press he owned. He sold the printing press in 1877 for $18,000, but prior to the sale, he printed one last issue with a statewide call convening Baptist deacons to meet him in Paris, Texas, for a deacon's convention. There he addressed the assembly and posed this one challenging question given the context of the ravages of the Civil War on families: "What if it was you that was dead, and your children left behind; what would you want the church to do?" That day he raised $200 and was challenged to raise another $1,800 so he could begin a children's home.

By 1879 Buckner had raised a total of $1,200, $800 short of the $2,000 goal. He decided to add $800 of his own money to get to $2,000 and started the Buckner Orphans Home in Dallas, Texas, at the corner of Junius and Haskell in a rented home where he and Vienna took in the first orphans. By 1880 he purchased forty acres at the corner of Buckner and Samuell in far east Dallas where the campus remains today. In 2019 we celebrated 140 years of ministry among vulnerable children, orphans, families, and seniors. The ministry extends across Texas and six countries, including Peru, Honduras, Guatemala, Mexico, the Dominican Republic, and Kenya, impacting hundreds of thousands of lives annually.

This would be a fantastic story if that were all there was to tell. Dr. Buckner not only started the Buckner Orphans Home, but he also started the Dallas Humane Society. He was a founding board member of the Baptist Sanitorium, which later became Baylor Hospital, now Baylor Scott & White. He started the first orphanage for African American children in Gilmer, Texas, the first African American Baptist Association, and the first graduate theological school for women. He wrote the first child labor laws for Texas and testified in Washington, D.C., to shape the federal child labor laws. All the while he remained an evangelist, pastor, preacher, church planter, and denominational leader until the very end. He preached to the orphans and told them about Jesus and His saving power. He baptized children and preached revivals. He started churches and established a church on the Buckner campus. He served his community from both sides of the coin—both preaching and doing the gospel. He brought the kingdom near. He brought solutions to social problems to orphans and widows who struggled by bringing peace, healing, and justice to bear on their lives.

Here is my point to the next generation. Dr. Buckner saw what was in the Word and had a vision to see it in the world, in his world. He was convicted with the witness of Scripture and moved to do something about it for his community, society, and state. He saw his community and knew what he had to do. So look at your world, then look at the Word, and discover a vision for the world that God will give you. Buckner had a motto he lived and served by: "Good words, good works, and good will." He chose his words carefully as if to live by the verse written by the Apostle Paul, "Do not let any unwholesome talk come out of your mouths but only what is helpful for building others up according to their needs, that it may benefit those who listen" (Ephesians 4:29). He focused on good works. To this day I can't figure out how he did it all. How could one man do so much? He must have been driven by the example of the Good Samaritan who Jesus talked about. He must have memorized, "As long as it is day, we must do the works of him who sent me. Night is coming, when no one can work" (John 9:4). He seemed to offer good will. He discriminated against no one. He acted from a position of goodwill to all. He focused on good intentions and good results for the benefit of others. "Good words, good works, and good will" is the perfect recipe for transforming a broken world and bringing the kingdom near. "Good words, good works, and good will" shines hope and brings peace, healing, and justice. It's what the world needs now.

BUCKNER INTERNATIONAL

Who We Are

Buckner International is a Christian ministry dedicated to the transformation and restoration of the lives we serve. As a Christ-centered organization, we deliver redemptive ministry to the most vulnerable from the beginning to the ending of life.

Whom We Serve

Motivated by the teachings and example of Jesus, we transform the lives of vulnerable children and orphans, enrich the lives of senior adults, and build strong families through Christ-centered values.

Why We Serve

We are driven by teaching in James 1:27 that says, "Religion that God our Father accepts as pure and faultless is this: to look after orphans and widows in their distress and to keep oneself from being polluted by the world." We follow Jesus into the villages, communities, and cities where the most vulnerable live. We shine the hope that is found in Christ. We partner with government agencies, churches, and volunteers in the US and abroad.

How We Serve

Founded in 1879, we are the oldest children's charity in Dallas, focusing our work among vulnerable children, orphans, families, and seniors. We provide three major services among children: foster care and adoption, Family Pathways, and Family Hope Centers. We have placed 1,100 children in foster care and 150 children in forever families through adoption in Texas. We also provide foster care and adoptive services and support internationally. Family Pathways is a program serving single mothers to gain independence and economic sustainability in collaboration with colleges and universities to equip them for vocation and family health. Family Hope Centers are places where struggling families are strengthened and supported from a strengths-based model featuring protective factors all families need to succeed. We serve seniors at Life Plan Communities featuring independent living, assisted living, skilled nursing, and memory care at six locations in Texas.

How You Can Help

Partnering with Buckner International provides tangible ways to bring the kingdom near, to shine hope, and to bring peace, healing, and justice to those we serve. We need volunteers to serve children and families. You may wish to volunteer in your community, conduct a shoe drive, sort shoes, deliver shoes, or contribute financially through our programs. To find out more about how you can help, visit www.buckner.org.

ACKNOWLEDGMENTS

An endeavor like writing a book is obviously not the work of one person. I have enjoyed the support of my wife Dr. Belinda Reyes and our sons, Joshua, David, and Thomas. Thanks for your encouragement and for listening to me talk about this book and for providing your feedback. The Buckner International Board of Trustees so graciously allowed me to take a sabbatical with financial support to travel to the Oxford Centre for Mission Studies in Oxford, England, to research the foundations of this book. I am indebted to the guidance of Dr. E. David Cook while writing this book. He is the founder of the Whitefield Institute in Oxford, England. I am grateful to Dr. Daniel R. Sanchez, professor of missions at Southwestern Baptist Theological Seminary for recommending a post-doctoral tutorial with Dr. E. David Cook at the Oxford Centre for Mission Studies as a potential destination for my sabbatical leave.

Serving Buckner International is a 24/7 proposition, 365 days a year. Serving over 400,000 children, families, and seniors through 1,400 staff in Texas and 1,000 affiliated nongovernment organization staff in six countries requires the best of leadership. Due to a gracious sabbatical period provided by the Buckner International board, the ministry was led by the able hands of Tony Lintelman, senior vice president of administration and chief financial officer. Our operational leaders, Henry Jackson, senior vice president of Buckner Children and Family Services, and Charlie Wilson, senior vice president of Buckner Retirement Services, led these organizations magnificently while launching major ministries. Arnie Adkison, vice president of development for Buckner International, led the resource acquisition effort at Buckner International with excellence.

Scott Collins, vice president of communications, encouraged me to write this book. Scott, thanks for your vision for publishing and lifting the Buckner brand. Steve Wakefield, vice president and general counsel, interjected plenty of dry humor to keep us guessing if he was serious or not. Steve, your wise counsel and steadiness provided a powerful sense of confidence in all we did at Buckner. Margaret Elizabeth McKissack, senior advisor for strategic initiatives, did an outstanding job leading strategic plan implementation and a wide variety of initiatives along with Glynnis Barrett, executive assistant to the CEO and special projects. During the second year of this project, two outstanding leaders joined my executive leadership team: Renee Reimer became our new vice president and general counsel replacing Steve Wakefield in 2018. Renee brings impressive expertise in legal services, risk management, and human resources and has proven to be an incredible addition to our team. Jeff Gentry joined us as senior vice president of financial services and chief financial officer. Jeff's experience in financial services and foster care is an outstanding addition to our team, replacing Tony Lintelman in late 2017.

ABOUT THE AUTHOR

Albert L. Reyes is the sixth president and CEO of Buckner International. He is a native of Corpus Christi, Texas. He became president of Buckner Children and Family Services Inc. in 2007, president of Buckner International in 2010, and president and CEO of Buckner International in 2012. Prior to service at Buckner International, he served as the sixth president of Baptist University of the Américas. His leadership experience over the past thirty years also includes telecom service management, military chaplaincy, and pastoral ministry.

Albert earned a bachelor of business administration degree in management from Angelo State University, a master of divinity degree and doctor of ministry degree in missiology from Southwestern Baptist Theological Seminary, and a doctor of philosophy degree in leadership from Andrews University. He has participated in executive management at the Harvard Kennedy School of Government and post-doctoral study at the Oxford Centre for Mission Studies in Oxford, England.

He served as president of the Baptist General Convention of Texas in 2004 and currently serves as vice president of the North American Baptist Fellowship, a regional fellowship of the Baptist World Alliance. He serves on the boards of the Christian Alliance for Orphans, National Hispanic Christian Leadership Conference, Both Ends Believing, and Stark College and Seminary. Albert and his wife Belinda have three adult sons, Joshua, David, and Thomas, and are members of Park Cities Baptist Church in Dallas.

If you enjoyed this book, will you consider sharing the message with others?

Let us know your thoughts at info@ironstreammedia.com. You can also let the author know by visiting or sharing a photo of the cover on our social media pages or leaving a review at a retailer's site. All of it helps us get the message out!

Facebook.com/IronStreamMedia

Iron Stream Books, New Hope® Publishers, Ascender Books, and New Hope Kidz are imprints of Iron Stream Media, which derives its name from Proverbs 27:17, "As iron sharpens iron, so one person sharpens another."

This sharpening describes the process of discipleship, one to another. With this in mind, Iron Stream Media provides a variety of solutions for churches, ministry leaders, and nonprofits ranging from in-depth Bible study curriculum and Christian book publishing to custom publishing and consultative services. Through our popular Life Bible Study, Student Life Bible Study brands, and New Hope imprints, ISM provides web-based full-year and short-term Bible study teaching plans as well as printed devotionals, Bibles, and discipleship curriculum.

For more information on ISM and Iron Stream Books, please visit

IronStreamMedia.com